W9-COP-564

The Great Buck Caper

And Other Tales from the North Country

The Great Buck Caper

And Other Tales from the North Country

David W. Hoffman

Edited by Jim Casada

The Great Buck Caper and Other Tales from the North Country

Published by Camby Outdoor Press

©Copyright 2004 by David W. Hoffman

International Standard Book Number (ISBN) 0-9754795-0-4

Printed in the United States of America by Bang Printing

10 9 8 7 6 5 4 3 2

For information:

Camby Outdoor Press • 12186 North Paddock Road • Camby, IN 46113

Library of Congress Control Number
2004094059

Dedicated to the Memory of Bob,
and to Cory and Reil.
Each lives on as a legend
in the North Country.

Contents

Foreword

Today's sporting world, and the sportsmen who congregate in it, seems obsessed with subjects such as "how to" and "where to," trophy bucks and record-breaking achievements. That's a crying shame. Think back (if you are old enough, and if you aren't, take a delightful trek down darkening avenues into the literature of America's sporting past) to the heyday of such sporting scribes as Nash Buckingham and Havilah Babcock, Gordon MacQuarrie and Archibald Rutledge, Corey Ford and Robert Ruark. Those individuals and others of their ilk understood that it wasn't filled limits or non-stop action that mattered most. Other considerations, while less tangible, were far more meaningful.

Who can fail to be enchanted by Nash Buckingham's enduring tales of waterfowling along the Mississippi Flyway with his staunch dark companion, Horace? Who can read Gordon MacQuarrie's timeless accounts of the Old Duck Hunters and think anything other than "Boy, I sure would have liked to be a part of that group?" Similarly, to read Archibald Rutledge's account of deer and turkey hunting is to take a wonderful adventure into a world we have largely lost, while both Havilah

Babcock and Corey Ford wrote with such power that they leave you misty-eyed one moment and laughing uncontrollably the next.

Most of all, there's the individual I personally consider our greatest American sporting scribe, Robert Ruark. He was a miserable S. O. B. in person, as I try to make clear in an anthology of his material I edited entitled "The Lost Classics of Robert Ruark." But when it came to capturing the essence of the sporting experience, the "Old Man's Boy" was in a class by himself. To read his accounts of lovingly prepared camp meals is to set one's salivary glands into overdrive, and to accompany him on something as simple as a Dixie dove hunt or as dangerous and exotic as a big game safari is to know vicarious hunting at its best.

Dave Hoffman understands, with a sure feel and distinctive flair, what all of these great writers knew. He realizes that considerations such as the people you meet, the friends you make, the closeness you attain to the land and the oneness with the wild world that you hope to achieve are the most important aspects of the sporting experience. We've all heard the overworked and often trite phrase, "that's what it is all about." Hoffman never uses that hackneyed linkage of words, but rest assured he understands the deeper meanings of sport.

Insofar as I can tell, and I read all these pieces with an editor's critical eye as well as for simple pleasure, everything that follows is drawn, in greater or lesser measure, from real life. I doubt if Hoffman ever encountered the old Southern phrase, "'tis a poor piece of cloth that can use no embroidery," but I'll venture to guess that he indulges in some literary stitching from time. That isn't a criticism. Far from it, for any storyteller worth his salt knows how to embellish and modify in a way that catches his audience's attention.

Moreover, true storytellers speak or write from the heart, and the love, respect, admiration, and emotion underlying these pieces runs as a bright, sparkling thread through the entire fabric of this book. Everyone who has hunted and fished a lot with a group of buddies will identify with some of the main characters of this book, and what a quaint, endearing lot they are – the Fearless Leader and his son, Moose Rider, the queen of cellulite, and a host of others.

Join them in these chronicles of adventure and misadventure in the North Country. You will laugh a lot, cry a little, and increasingly recognize that the gladness and occasional sadness that spice these pages are a reflection of the truly good life. Not a life based on material wealth or grand achievement, but rather one of simpler days and simpler ways. You will find these tales rewarding, meaningful and, most of all, an exercise in the most pleasant sort of armchair adventure. If I may end on a personal note, I also found them significant in one other way. It's heartening to know that storytelling as it relates to sport is not quite yet a lost art.

Jim Casada
Past President
Outdoor Writers Association of America

Acknowledgements

I am deeply grateful to the many people who have inspired me to write this book. Especially the Fearless Leader, his family and the troops who followed him into the North Country woods. Thanks to the SES coterie, the Manitou sporting set and the many friends with whom it has been an exciting adventure to accompany afield.

I learned to read about and to enjoy wildlife at an early age; I've learned to write only recently. I would like to thank the Keeper of Clichés who improved my writing style. Generous assistance in reviewing the early drafts of the collection of stories was provided by readers: Bill Beck of Lakeside Writers' Group, Brandon Hoffman, Lew Liggett, and Ahto Niemioja. Thanks to Susan S. Yoke for preparing the illustrations and a special thanks to Trudy Calvert for the portrait of our Fearless Leader and the cover illustration. I owe a debt of gratitude to Mary Johnson who helped me out, as she has done so many times, by proofreading the final copy. Scott "The Machine" Ritchie demonstrated his creative talents in producing the cover design and layout, and guided me throughout the production process. Jim Casada, a veteran of many such endeavors, skillfully edited the manuscript and provided much helpful guidance. To all I am truly indebted.

"Our Fearless Leader"

The Great Buck Caper

It was that supreme season of the year when the best of friends revert to youth.

Opening weekend of deer season was upon the great North Country. Our cherished Fearless Leader had directed our amicable hunting party through a day-and-a-half of military-like maneuvers across the entire snow-covered county to no avail. We hadn't even seen a buck, much less shoot at one, and the pressure was mounting.

In our little town, competition during hunting season was fierce, and egos were the high stakes. Strangely, it was as if there were some correlation between the size of one's buck and the hunters' testosterone level.

You see, there is this long-standing bet between the Fearless Leader and his boyhood hunting buddy Moose Rider. The biggest buck taken on opening weekend and the biggest of the deer season are good for a case of beer, compliments of the loser. Of course, local deerslayers follow the traditional challenge as closely as a daytime soap opera, and the score sheet dates back many years. The drama concludes at the Fearless Leader's homey tavern on Sunday evenings amid much fanfare and hoopla. It's a scene witnessed throughout the North Country.

Only four hours of frail November daylight remained before the traditional rendezvous at the tavern to swap stories and determine who had earned the opening weekend bragging rights and the cold brewskies. What if the Fearless Leader's entire troop showed up empty-handed for opening weekend? No doubt howls of laughter would spread like wildfire around the congenial tavern and our small town.

"This doesn't look good, boys," moaned our Fearless Leader. "I've got to come up with a new plan." Following a brief thoughtful pause, he added, "I think I'll call it Plan B for bucks." I saw a weak smile develop as he checked his watch then pulled a couple of black bungee cords from behind the worn seat of his aging pickup truck.

That familiar uneasy feeling returned to my stomach. I knew he was desperate, and I knew that I would somehow be included in the Fearless Leader's infamous Plan B. But I didn't have a clue what he was thinking.

He had earned his nickname during an intense party after a Packer victory over the Minnesota Vikings. He lay crumpled on his living room couch – a victim of whisky Manhattans – which he only consumed when he knew for sure that he was going to win. A single snapshot had been taken as he lay there beside a half empty bottle of Canadian Club. That picture was strategically hung in the sport shop and was inscribed "Our Fearless Leader" by someone with poor penmanship.

The nickname stuck; after all, he was a natural-born leader. Although he didn't learn much in college, he got a good education during his four years in the Air Force. Returning to the North Country, he managed the restaurant, tavern and sport shop for his aging father, a quiet, distant soul, who always wore a dark green uniform like the old auto mechanics. Although our Fearless Leader had the same stocky frame and stiff walk of the old man, he was gregarious, dressed in the latest sport clothes and was active in the town's many community organizations and activities.

Hunting and fishing at every opportunity as he grew up in the North Country, our Fearless Leader had numerous fish and game birds mounted by the local taxidermist. His stories about each of the trophies were embellished over the years as he felt the pressure to live up to his reputation as our leader. But he was human and had been known to succumb to temptation. There was the time he hunted a prime-looking brushy field within the city limits of a nearby town, the name of which I shall not mention. Approached by the authorities shortly after the successful hunt began, he swiftly pitched the two pheasants he had downed into the weeds. Unfortunately, but much to the delight of the warden, his trusty black Lab sniffed the birds out and returned to drop them at his feet. For a while he considered renaming the Lab from Cricket to Ticket. He has a way of always making light of the situation at hand.

But deer season had not been kind, and time was running out. As I suspected, he divided up the troops. Avis, Jackson, Chip and Wild Man went west on Old Highway A; Russ, Eddie-John, Scottie and Kamikaze drove down to a secluded, rugged and productive area we called "Swamp Angels." Many fine bucks were taken there each season. Moe and the Gentle Warrior would park their truck somewhere, drink coffee and hope for a minor miracle.

"Doc and I are going to see if we can jump that big buck that's been coming into the Anderson's feeder, then head out to Hopewell's farm," said our Captain.

"Why go out there?" asked Avis. "Ain't nothin' out there 'cept a few does."

"Trust me," answered our Fearless Leader. I knew right away that he had all the confidence in the world behind Plan B.

The troops admired his determination, although they never knew what he would do to get a shot at a big buck. There are countless tales of his mischief-making and prowess circulating around the North Country. Many of them are true.

"We'll meet you guys at the DNR check station at sundown and then go over to the tav-ern," asserted our leader as we departed. He had a unique way of saying "tavern" by breaking it into two equally enunciated parts.

He cranked the engine of the brown Chevy pickup, and we headed for the woods, bypassing the Anderson's feeder without slowing down. I doubted that we would shoot a deer that was coming to a local resident's feeder, but one never knew. He did love to hunt and hated to lose a bet. I wondered if Plan B was about to commence.

"I've seen a couple of fat beauties hanging around the corner of Hopewell's clover field where the power line crosses," he said. "But first we have to stop by your house. There's something I need out of your workshop," he said as he glanced at me with his dimples showing deeply. Something was up.

After a quick visit to my workshop, we approached Hopewell's and parked the pickup in a small jackpine plantation. We then followed the power line into a field hidden from view of all of the surrounding roads. Grazing nervously were two heavy, mature does which were about to receive a lot of attention. The hunt was easy, and we were on our way with the two plump animals in the pickup bed with two hours still remaining before meeting the rest of the illustrious hunting party at the check station.

"Let's stop and have a brewski, Doc," he said as he began to grin. "I think I might even be feeling a Manhattan coming on later," he added as he parked the truck at a spot overlooking the scenic Gordon Flowage. The dendritic pattern of the bare deciduous tree branches looked like maps of expansive river systems, and they stood out against a sky that ranged from pink near the horizon to dark blue directly overhead. Accumulating groups of clouds were gray on top and reflected the pink of the sky underneath as they drifted rapidly from the northwest. A snow-shoe hare, having completed its color transition from brown to almost completely white, scampered nearby and hurriedly fed on nutritious buds while leaving its characteristic chisel cut on the ends of the stems. We sipped the cold liquid and talked of past adventures. North Country adventures.

"Remember that time when we went to the Big Two-Hearted River in the UP?" he asked. "We should go deer huntin' over there sometime."

"Sure, I remember that," I responded. "I remember every-thing having to do with fishing for brook trout." It was true.

We had both read Hemingway and took the pilgrimage to the Big Two-Hearted River and fished it as he had. However, we stopped short of eating a frying pan full of pork and beans mixed with spaghetti from a can. The same goes for the sliced onion sandwiches that Papa described in specific detail.

"No wonder he was a cantankerous old guy," I remarked to the Fearless Leader. "If he ate the kind of chow that he described in his book, he must have had a lot of digestive problems and gas."

"That's for sure!" chuckled our leader as he looked at his watch for the third time in the last 10 minutes. I could tell his mind was busy thinking about something. I was certain that it wasn't literature.

"You know," he finally said, "I think I'll just tell the rest of 'em to meet us at the tav-ern instead of the check station." Part of Plan B, no doubt!

He reached for the CB radio. "Doc and I hit the jackpot!" he shouted to the rest of the troops. "Go straight over to the tav-ern and tell everybody that Doc is dropping me off in about an hour." I winced. He smiled.

The Fearless Leader got out and worked on his plan for a minute, then jumped back in with a deep grin. He popped open another beer while we continued to discuss deer hunting. We marveled at a buck's unique ability to recognize, from a great distance, whether or not a person represents any threat of danger. And the older a buck gets, the smarter and warier he becomes.

"People used to say that hunting from a tree stand was the ultimate since a buck would never look up," he lamented. "That isn't true anymore. No doubt about it, they're getting smarter. They even figured out our drives. I saw them sneaking off the back corner of that last drive as soon as they heard the truck doors close. There are lots of weird things going on in the woods these days," he chuckled. I was quick to agree.

Afternoon clouds were giving way to darkness, and a light snow began to fall. Chickadees ceased their joyous refrain as twilight approached. I knew that Plan B was about to unfold.

"Perfect conditions," he finally exclaimed as darkness permeated the cab of the pickup. "Now let's get this show on the road."

I felt as uneasy as usual during these adventures, but the beer helped instill a sense of confidence. Besides, I knew I had to go through with it to protect the Fearless Leader's reputation. I put my blaze orange hat back on my head and lowered the battered tailgate so that the deer could easily be seen, then slid behind the wheel of his pickup.

Arriving in town, we pulled onto County Road A, which was dimly lit and tree lined, and approached the tavern's east window. As I expected, 20 or more faces were peering out of the neon-framed window into the darkness as the jukebox was blasting out a country and western song about friends in low places. Stopping the truck, I shifted down to first gear, then honked the horn several times.

Jumping from the cab, our leader pointed to the deer in the truck bed and gestured with his hands on either side of his head to symbolize big antlers. As orange-clad figures began to pour into the darkened street, his shouts and laughter could be heard above the noise. I waited only long enough so that the first ones out of the tavern could briefly see the two deer in the dim light, but not long enough for them to get too close to the truck. I released the clutch when I heard the Fearless Leader proclaim, "More whiskey!" I concluded that someone told him that he had won the case of beer from Moose Rider. Turning the corner onto the highway and accelerating, I glanced back at the deer and chuckled to myself. I knew that we had pulled it off. Yes!

Before driving to the pole barn to hang the deer, I stopped by my house, removed the Fearless Leader's bungee cords that held the 12-point and 14-point sets of antlers to the heads of the hapless does, and returned the antlers to their shelf in my workshop. I didn't get to hear the tales told and retold at the "tav-ern" that night, but it didn't matter. By morning the stories of our two "monster bucks" would be all over town.

Did You Get Your Deer?

Did you get your deer? I'd like to have a nickel for every time someone asks that question during deer season in the North Country. I can't recall a season that I haven't heard it at least a dozen times or more. Lately, I've spent a lot of time trying to figure out what's really behind that incessant question.

First of all, how do you tell which deer is yours? To be honest, I wouldn't know how to go about making such a determination, and I doubt that any respectable buck would stand still long enough for any sort of examination. Certainly, I haven't noticed any deer running around in the woods with people's names showing anywhere that was visible. Could it be that I just haven't been looking in the right places?

Heck! Each time I had the opportunity to take a deer, I never stopped to think twice about whether or not it was mine. I was usually so excited when I had the chance; I just went ahead and shot. Was that a mistake?

Since I didn't know if the buck was mine, I couldn't tell if I should have felt guilty about shooting someone else's deer or not. Maybe I was supposed to lie awake at night feeling guilt-ridden, or perhaps I should have considered going to church and fessing-up. I don't know.

Conceivably, the question is just an "ice breaker," a non-threatening way of beginning conversations like talking about the weather. Or possibly it's like when someone asks you, "How are you doing?" and you know that particular person really couldn't care less if you were about to croak. But mark my word, as soon as deer season begins people around the office start asking, "Did you get your deer?" Are they genuinely interested or is it just small talk?

Come to think of it, there **must** be more meaning behind the question than that! I've even heard my wife and a lot of other friends ask the question at the grocery store, during bingo, and at church potluck suppers. Seems strange to me that most of these folks don't hunt or particularly care about hunting.

Furthermore, many deer season widows don't like to eat or even cook venison. In fact, the only thing most of them like about deer season is getting the old man out of the house for a week. So why do **they** ask this question? Could it be a one-upmanship; or in this case, a one-upwomanship thing? Does a deer widow only ask the question, "Did your husband get his deer?" after her own husband has harvested one? Maybe that's the game. Perhaps it's played something like this:

"So! Did your husband get his deer?"

"Oh geez! Not yet."

"Oh, that's too bad."

"Did your husband get his deer?"

"Oh geez! He did, as a matter of fact. It was a nice six-pointer. Maybe your husband will have better luck tomorrow."

"Oh! I hope so. And be sure to tell your husband congratulations." (As she thinks to herself, "And also tell the beer guzzling, chauvinistic goat it was probably just a lucky shot.")

I have my suspicions about the motive behind this recurrent question, and I guess it will be repeated in the North Country as long as we maintain the right to bear arms. Whatever the case, I think I have the right answer. I've suggested to my wife that when someone asks, "Did your husband get his deer?" she should respond: "No, but he did get someone else's, and he was elated because it was a hell of a lot bigger than his!"

Stag Pyrexia

Peering around the mossy oak tree with mixed curiosity and concern was a regal white-tailed buck. As he jerked his head high, it seemed like his massive rack contained a gazillion antler tines – maybe more. The denizen of the Northern Michigan forest looked directly at the hunter who was forthwith rendered helpless. His throat constricted, then his breathing ceased, and his heart threatened to burst.

One is unlikely to recognize the first subtle hints of stag pyrexia. It may only be an instantaneous dilation of the pupils that spreads with the speed of a frightened doe.

Tightening of the chest cavity and an inability to breathe normally are the most notable of the early warning signs. By then it is too late – you've got it bad. In fact, it begins to feel like one's diaphragm has stopped functioning. Breath comes to sluggish lungs with great difficulty, and fear spreads like wildfire. There is a dread that the interrupted airflow and forced breathing will give away one's location and that buck of a lifetime will vanish. It may do just that!

The larger the buck's antlers, the higher the dose of searing adrenaline shooting into the circulatory system, and the more one's ears pound as the blood pressure soars. Within chest walls the heart races frantically, seemingly loud enough to be audible 100 yards away. Jumbled thoughts suggest the concept of heart failure to the message centers of older hunters. Tension builds.

Cotton turns the mouth into an instant desert. Incoherent thoughts get jumbled in the numb brain. Neurons fire and misfire. Caution and skill lock in a valiant struggle with panic for control of the senses.

"Don't move! He'll see you!" shouts logic.

"Shoot quickly before he gets away!" pleads desire.

Lightheadedness may even develop, and the horrifying thought of fainting and falling out of a deer stand emerges in the minds of some hunters. If the fall doesn't kill you, the embarrassment may when the stories are told at deer camp.

The solid steadiness with which one held the deer gun during practice cannot be duplicated. Are you kidding? Estimating the distance to the trophy deer to calculate projectile drop over distance defies comprehension in such a panicked instant. Aim and shoot! Now!

The soul pleads, "Stand still! Please don't run." Fear of disappointment and loss collides head-on with optimism. Success versus failure. Shoot, man!

Don't panic! Get a grip on yourself, for physiological and chemical reactions are cascading through the veins and muscles. Knees weaken and breathing comes and goes as choppy as a wild pickup ride down a washboard road as one takes aim and pleads, "Please! Please!" There is hope and desperation. Fear and joy ... and more desperation.

They tell one to relax and concentrate, squeeze the trigger gradually. Hold it steady and choose your shot with care. Right!

Be confident. Practice lots. Be prepared and it won't happen. Sure!

Call it "stag pyrexia" or call it "buck fever." We all recognize it, and we all know that it has a heartless, relentless grip. It comes in varying degrees of intensity, to be sure. But it afflicts all deer hunters, amateur or pro. Yes, it is an infirmity that attacks the unsuspecting, the unskilled, the experienced and just about everyone else in between. Insidious as cancer, it is a disorder inherent in hunting for deer. Especially monster bucks!

Though most deer hunters whom I know vehemently deny being stricken, I dare say it has afflicted all of us to some degree, especially when that monster buck suddenly appears from nowhere and raises its massive antlered head and stares directly into one's eyes. It'll get to you! You've been there, haven't you?

"And you know what, Doc?" said Avis, my long-time deer hunting partner. "The day I don't get excited at the sight of a big buck looking around the tree at me – that's the day I quit hunting deer."

Well said, Avis.

First Bow Hunt

Constructed in a picture postcard setting by a tree-lined lake in Douglas County, the rustic log home was more than 50 years old. Although it needed skillful restoration that would be expensive, the old place had a lot of character. As far as I was concerned, the benefits of living deep in the North Country were appealing, especially the opportunities for autumn bow hunting. But it was a northern pike instead of a white-tailed deer that closed the home-buying deal.

Living in a pleasant rural setting was adequate, but there was a certain emptiness about our home place located in a mature birch and aspen forest. Shopping around for lake property on previous occasions yielded nothing that satisfied our interests. But then that rascal called. He said he had what we were looking for, and that started the chain of events that led to my most memorable bow hunt.

He had started selling property after he decided that the financial benefits outweighed those of being the local mortician. Local deer hunters called him "Digger" – an obvious reference to his previous profession. And he was a darned good salesman as well – perhaps too good!

Believe me, I have often told the story of looking at the rustic old lodge a second and third time. Digger had suggested that the bride and I sit in the grand room in front of the fieldstone fireplace to get the feel of the lodge and to talk the deal over. Outside, he was arranging a fishing pole and spinner bait for our son who had become bored with our indecisiveness. Next thing we heard were excited shouts and a distinct cackle coming from the boat dock. Bent and waving like a reed in a November gale was Digger's spinning rod. He was at our son's shoulder coaching him on the fine art of fighting and landing a giant northern pike in one quick and easy lesson. Both the northern pike and our son had been hooked. We signed the papers that day!

Although I could never prove it, I was acutely suspicious that the pike event was somehow staged as a sale-closing technique, and I told Digger so. What an effective clincher! Therefore, I told that story as if it were true at every party and social event where I had the opportunity to do so in his presence, much to his delight! His shattering falsetto cackle could bring a smile to even the most stoic. And do you know what? The son-of-a-gun never denied having arranged the pike-catching, sale-closing strategy.

Since he was active in the Legion and Lions, as well as being a dedicated member of the town board, everyone in town knew Digger and his distinct, infectious laugh. A big man, with long salt and pepper sideburns and friendly eyes, he was a shrewd businessman. He played cards with a passion. His appetite was voracious – he could really put away the chow – especially on someone else's nickel. Stress and other factors of his chaotic lifestyle had taken their toll on his health, and he was supposed to slow down, although he seldom did. Especially when it came to hunting deer. Feeling I was somehow being suckered in; I accepted his offer to introduce me to bow hunting on one of the secluded properties that he owned. It was all his fault, you see.

Isolated in the middle of a section within the Gordon Quadrangle was the secret hunting site. Access was gained by an old logging road which was reached by driving around to the backside of an abandoned gravel pit. In the fall, the pit was utilized by a few of the local deer hunters to sight in their deer rifles. Otherwise, few people wandered through the property. It looked like a perfect spot to stick a careless buck. "Plus," advised Digger with a sly cackle, "it just happens to be for sale."

Driving past the pit and onto the property, we could see deer signs before we stopped the vehicle. Digger got out and directed my attention to a fresh buck rub on a six-inch maple located at the far end of the woods where an old homestead once existed. Growing in a straight row were three apple trees that undoubtedly once served as a food source for the inhabitants and now provided a source of mast for the deer. They stood as a living monument to a failed attempt to farm the area. We located four well-used game trails, likely those of a doe family unit. Circular depressions of matted grasses gave away their bedding area deep within the confines of the property. Flowing from a nearby spring was an ample supply of icy cold water. What a setup! In spite of it being the only scouting trip I had conducted before hunting opener approached, my hopes for a successful bow hunt were heightened.

Bow hunting to me is a mighty good excuse to get out of the office and enjoy the fall splendor. It's that special time of year when the Maker of Frost paints the woods with a brilliant palette and covers it with white and transparent crystals in the early hours of the morning. When the crystals melt under a cobalt sky of autumn, men and women of the North Country are inspired to take to the woods in search of grouse, deer and themselves. A sense of excitement and urgency prevails. My frantic hunting preparations were well underway.

Practicing faithfully on a foam target every night, I became proficient and a reasonable judge of distance. I knew my effective shooting range was 30 yards, and I felt confident that "buck fever" would not interfere with my goal of taking a buck if presented the opportunity. A monster buck would be great, but any buck would do, even a button buck. He would be my first with a bow.

The outdoors seemed to call to me as I drove to and from work where I had trouble concentrating that week. Inviting sights and sounds of autumn beckoned, and I could hardly wait until the weekend. I had made an appointment in my official office calendar for a day in the woods instead of my usual week-end office visits. No paperwork for me, no reports, no meetings, no phone calls. The weekend agenda was going to be different. I was going bow hunting.

Easing the dew-covered pickup out of the driveway on that magical, long-awaited Saturday morning, I departed while most of the little town slept. The boardroom in the woods was my destination, and my only appointment was a tentative one with a wary buck. The strategy was solid, and I had confidence in my shooting ability, although I had to admit that the probability of arrowing a buck on the first day of bow hunting was pretty darned low. But I had beaten the odds before. It seemed like part of my daily job at the office. I was committed.

As I slowed the pickup to make the turn off of the county road, three whitetails bounded elegantly across the road and entered the woods in a single file. In the dim light of the morning, I couldn't tell how many were does or bucks. However, they were deer and they had moved gracefully, not appearing to be highly alarmed. I knew that deer typically leave their night feeding areas early in the morning and move to dense cover to bed down. Since their tails had remained low, not high and waving to indicate danger, I assumed they were heading toward a bedding area. Having a four-chambered stomach, deer chew their cud in the safety of cover after feeding during the night and drinking in the early morning.

At least the deer were moving in the direction of my selected hunting site, although much sooner than I desired. To have any opportunity for a shot, I would have to drive down the trail that ran parallel to their direction of travel. Their keen senses would surely be alert to my every move. I realized they would follow my forward progress with their heads held high; their ears erect and cocked forward. Should I keep going as planned or should I give it up? It could be a futile exercise, but I decided to continue. What the heck!

Bucking along the trail in the pickup, I tried to hurry to get well in front of the nimble trio. Shutting off the engine where the trail ended, I fought a sudden twinge of panic. I would have to move fast like a hungry wolf positioning himself to ambush the prey. My senses were charged.

Uncasing the bow, I got out of the truck and hurried ahead in my desperate attempt to head them off. My heart began to quicken, and I felt as rushed as if I had a critical budget deadline to meet at the office. Carrying the bow through the brush surrounding the woods was something I hadn't practiced. Never thought of it! So there I went thrashing through the underbrush and catching the bow on limbs as well as snapping twigs and rustling leaves beneath my boots. I had wanted to silently position myself in front of them, but I must have sounded more like a giant Sasquatch crashing through the forest!

Sneaking in front of the deer without being detected was out of the question, and I thought I might as well give it up. With all of the undesirable racket, I figured there was little chance of getting close to even the most careless or decrepit deer. However, before I gave up, I decided to use my grunting tube once or twice since it was my newest hunting gadget. I had purchased it on a whim. Practice grunts were attempted in the privacy of my basement, but I had never tested it in the field. Maybe the deer would be gullible enough to think a monster buck was exerting its dominance by making all the branch-breaking and leaf-rustling noises. Who knows? Every experienced deer hunter I know tells me that strange things happen during deer season. I eased the ribbed plastic tube to my mouth, and although I was out of breath, gave it a soft blow.

A grunting sound was immediately repeated as if there were an echo in the forest. But the sound came from behind me. A young forky had observed my struggle though the brush, and I had passed within 25 yards of where he stood. Heck, he wasn't even bedded down in the long grasses attempting to blend with his surroundings like they do so well. He was just standing there like a bronze statue. Eyeing me with curiosity, he raised and lowered his head; his ears were forward but his tail was not raised in alarm. Perhaps he was trying to figure out how one person could make so much racket stumbling through the bush. Or perhaps he really **had** expected to see a giant Sasquatch!

Stories told of cagey old bucks that stand motionless allowing hunters to pass within a few yards are true, as many veteran hunters can attest. But what are you supposed to do? Freeze? Slowly or hastily try to nock an arrow and shoot? I chose the slow approach, although my heart was beating to the proverbial beat of a different drummer. I eased the arrow into place as the buck continued to raise and lower his head and sniff the air searching for olfactory clues. His moist nostrils twitched and the white patch on his neck and inside his ears glowed faintly in the low morning sun.

Sucking in air, I pulled the aluminum arrow back while avoiding eye contact with the perky buck. I zeroed in on the vital area as I had done a hundred times in practice. Bow hunting wasn't supposed to be so easy! I hadn't been hunting for 15 minutes, but it was all falling into place. Or was this something that Digger had arranged like the northern pike incident? That rascal! Had he faked the buck rubs and bedding areas? Surely not!

Keeping the sighting pin glued to the buck's vitals, I released the arrow in one smooth motion. Covering the distance in a heartbeat the arrow stuck with a resounding and memorable thud. Leaping straight up in the air, the startled buck turned completely around. When he hit the ground, he didn't twitch. His eyes were wide open and frightened and fixed … on the arrow stuck in the elm tree above him. I stared at the arrow too, but in disbelief. It wasn't even close. What the hey? I couldn't have missed by such a huge distance with him standing broadside at 25 yards. Of course, before I could get another arrow nocked, my quarry trotted away unscathed, though perhaps puzzled by the calamity. My heart sank.

I had thought that buck fever was conquered. That must be one of its symptoms; you think that you are in control but you aren't at all. Still, I refused to believe that I had missed by such a large margin. He had been standing right there!

The ride home was filled with emotion. Mixed feelings of disappointment and of elation. It was a grunt in the woods to be remembered. I had seen a buck, and he had responded to my grunt tube, though not precisely in that order. I had gotten close enough to take a shot at a buck within 15 minutes on my first day bow hunting. That had to be considered a major success, and I was thrilled with the brief exciting adventure and rush of adrenaline.

Stopping by the real estate office, I knew Digger would be in early. Saturdays were busy. I related the whole story amid many hearty cackling outbursts from the former gravedigger. Voicing my suspicions that the incident had somehow been canned brought more unrestrained outbursts of laughter, although he didn't deny setting it up!

Rendering his diagnosis, Digger said, "Yep! Buck fever! No doubt about it, but you'll get lots of those chances out here, and you'll get over it eventually." The prognosis was bittersweet. "The good news," he said with a huge grin and a slight cackle, "is that the property is still for sale. Better grab it quick."

"You rascal, it's got to be another one of your sale-closing strategies," I said only half jokingly. "See ya later," I said and left the building and contemplated going to my office as usual.

I was still turning the events of the hunt over in my mind as I pulled the pickup off of the frontage road next to Highway 53 and onto the drive leading to the lodge. "How could that be?" I repeated out loud for the tenth time. As I reached the circle at the end of the drive, I knew in an instant how that could be. For lying in the driveway in front of the garage was one of my arrows. My son had found a new friend after we moved into the lodge, and his new pal had already been into mischief on three separate occasions. Theorizing they had taken my bow out for some unauthorized practice when I was at work, I figured they had readjusted the sighting pins. And my theory was correct!

Some of the most memorable hunts are unsuccessful. My first attempt at bow hunting was over. The buck was gone. But I was hooked on bow hunting for white-tailed bucks. Hooked as solidly as a big northern pike on a spinner bait!

Run, Dogie, Run!

It was a classic battle between desire and logic! What possesses a sportsman to do something wild, dangerous and perhaps a little crazy like wanting to ride an adult moose?

"Edge her in a little closer," he said, "speed her up a tad, too."

As the vintage 16-foot Lund swung near the swimming moose, he edged his sturdy right leg over the side. Thinking about the strength of the churning legs of the moose and the outboard's propeller, he paused as if he considered yielding to reason and logic. Adrenaline-primed muscles were ready to explode.

"That's good, now hold her there." His voice was firm and confident, yet he had to have had some reservations. Had to!

"Here we go!"

This collection of stories told at deer camp would not be complete without including the tale of how Moose Rider got his name. You would have to meet him to realize that the story is true. Yes, it really did happen, so let me begin by introducing this unique character. Now we all know sportsmen and women who go for the gusto; those outdoor types who are not content with the ordinary. Not misfits nor sociopaths, but those rare folks willing to risk it all for some strange reason. Such is Moose Rider who just happened to have grown up with our Fearless Leader. Their friendship and competitive spirits prevailed over many adventure-filled deer seasons. Many North Country tales are told about their exploits. What one wouldn't do, the other would.

"Don't know when that one started," admits Moose Rider. "But I had the idea I wanted to ride a full-grown moose. It may have originated as a story told to me by an old Canadian guide when I was a kid on one of our family fishing trips. Somehow I remember a story about a guy jumping from his canoe onto the back of a moose, and since he had a long way to go to shore, he tied his canoe's painter rope to the moose's antlers. Well, the moose hit the shallows near shore before the guy realized it, and that scared him. So he was bouncing up and down like a bronco rider and didn't get his rope loose before he jumped off. Last he saw of the moose it was high-tailing it through the bush, canoe in tow, and ricocheting off the aspens and the lichen-covered boulders like a tennis ball. The guy eventually found his canoe, but it was wrecked beyond use. He had to walk 16 miles around the lake to get back to camp. I can't recall for sure who told me the story, but I do know that I always wanted to take a moose ride. One other thing I know is that I'll be smart enough to get off before the moose hits the shore."

Believe me, the Moose Rider looks like the kind of guy who could ride a moose. Stout as a hardwood six-by-six, he spent most of his career operating the local bakery and teaching baking at the local junior college. Anyone who had spent time in the military learned that it is a good idea to befriend those who work in the bakery for two reasons. First, you may be able to get a couple extra rations on occasion. And, since they had to do all of their mixing of batter by hand, they were the strongest guys around.

All of that was years ago, and now he is starting to show a

distinct salt-and-pepper pattern in his thinning hair and bushy moustache. Standing over six feet and able bodied, he moves through the woods with the confidence and ease of a dominant buck.

Always in contention for the biggest buck, and one of the first guys out on the newly formed ice for lake trout, he will venture where no others go. And he does so with pride! More often than not he will wait until the last day of the season to take his big buck or pull the largest northern pike out of the frozen lake. That's why people who know him have no doubts about the tale of the moose-riding escapade.

Somewhere along the line he concluded that the one and only way to get on an adult moose was to climb aboard when one was swimming in the water. For six or seven spring Canadian fishing trips, he watched for an opportunity. However, the opportunity did not arise until three years ago.

"We were anchored near a shallow, rocky point fishing for walleyes, and it was getting to be a wicked evening with horseshit weather," he related in his direct pattern of speech. "There were two-foot high waves and the wind was pretty darned stiff out of the northwest." His brother, Bebe – my brook trout fishing partner – was running the boat motor. Another family friend from Montana was on board but had never heard of the crazy moose-riding desire.

"The whole thing began when Bebe saw the cow swimming along between a distant point and the far shore 600 or so yards away."

"Moose in the water!" shouted Bebe as he reached back to give the outboard a crank. Moose Rider hoisted the anchor without even looking around to see the moose and began pulling off his rain gear.

"He wants to do what?" questioned the bewildered first-timer from Montana. He turned his brand new baseball cap promoting the Calgary Stampede around on his head as the Lund gathered speed. "Is he out of his freaking mind or what?"

Spray flew and the boat rocked in the rough water. The fishing boat pulled alongside the moose like a tug boat meeting an ocean liner, and after ignoring a common sense plea from some primal response deep within his brain, he shouted, "Here we go!" Bobbing up and down next to the startled moose that had kicked into high gear, the boat was in position and the legendary Moose Rider eased onto the huge animal's back.

"Run, Dogie, Run!" shouted the North Country cowboy above the blowing wind in the open lake channel. "That was the only thing I could think of saying," he chuckled. "She turned her head around and looked at me, and her eye looked as big as a dinner plate. It was red, too, big and red." Off they went across the lake channel, but as the moose approached the shore, it turned around for some reason. Maybe it had heard a story from another moose. Anyway, she returned the same way she came, straight across the open choppy water toward the exact spot where she had entered the water. No one has ever claimed that moose are particularly bright animals.

Returning back across the channel chugged moose and man. Because of the wind, waves and drizzle, the moose jockey was getting chilled to the bone, and the adrenaline rush was wearing off. The moose was also getting tired of carrying the hitchhiker in his soggy wool clothes.

"She started grunting and getting nervous like she was running out of energy when she approached the other side. Plus, she was getting jittery and scared, so I just eased off of her back and watched her scramble up the shore with water spraying everywhere. She galloped off to beat hell into the spruce and disappeared," said the gratified Moose Rider as he recalled the unique event.

About this time he turned his attention toward the boat he expected to be at hand to pick him up. It was then he realized that the Lund was a good distance from him. He was feeling exhausted and perhaps a little hypothermic.

"Tell you one thing for sure," recalled Moose Rider, "you can't swim worth a hoot with hush puppies on your feet. Don't try that trick at home!"

Seeing the rescue team in the boat, it appeared to Moose Rider that they weren't looking for him. They were on their knees and appeared to be trying to get the boat started. Panic nearly engulfed him, but he managed to keep treading water. He later learned that they were indeed on their knees, laughing at the comical sight so hard they couldn't stand. What a sight it must have been! Of course, nobody had a camera so the event was not captured as a Kodak moment.

Moose Rider was finally pulled from the frigid, stinging water and taken back toward camp. Bebe and the other guy decided to return to their interrupted walleye fishing. They still needed three walleyes to fill their limit, and it was getting late. As they approached the rocky shore and their wet passenger jumped out of the boat into the turbulent flotsam, he slipped on a moss-covered rock and splashed into the surf once again. Recovering from the tumble, the water-soaked Moose Rider made his way back toward camp. He probably should not have been left alone but would have refused any assistance anyway.

He passed through the camp of four other friends who had traveled to Canada with his party. These guys were smart enough to have passed on the invitation to fish the last day and were, in fact, partying and playing cards. Of course, Moose Rider joined the party and held his audience captive while he excitedly told the story ... that no one believed. A couple of snorts of peppermint schnapps later, the shivering Moose Rider headed back to his own camp. Even before changing his soaked clothes, he blurted out the moose riding adventure to his companions. To his dismay, nobody there believed him either. Not that he was prone to exaggerate in the past!

"How the hell do you think I got so wet?" challenged Moose Rider.

"We saw you fall out of the boat into the water. You were flopping like a crappie. It looked to me like you just had too many brewskies and fell out of the boat, you animal," was the response from Gentleman Jim, a regular on these spring excursions.

"I couldn't believe they thought I had too many snorts and fell in the lake," recounted Moose Rider. He had accomplished a remarkable feat, a lifetime goal that few have attempted or achieved. And nobody believed him! There were no pictures to prove he had done it. Bebe and his buddy were camped on a small

island, so they could not corroborate the story. Exasperated, Moose Rider finally slipped into his down sleeping bag.

The following morning was bright and calm, and the skeptics jeered Moose Rider as they gathered at the predetermined spot for breakfast. "What did you ride in your sleep last night?" asked our Fearless Leader. "We heard you thrashing around all night," added Gentleman Jim, "sounded like you were saying something about riding dogs. It must be about time to head back to civilization. You've been in the woods too long."

Another party member shouted, "You've got a camera don't you? Where the heck are all the moose riding pictures? Riding a moose! That's the biggest hoax since the Piltdown man!"

The coffeepot was boiling furiously, and the cast iron skillet was warming over the wood-fueled fire as breakfast preparations were underway. Preparing fish fillets and slicing potatoes for cooking kept members of the party busy. Some were also trying to pack their fishing gear for the long trip back across the border. The memorable final meal of a successful fishing trip was approaching.

Bebe and his companion edged their Lund to shore to join the raucous group. They had gone out onto the lake early to catch the remaining walleyes still needed to fill everyone's limit. Securing the boat in haste, they turned and hurried to the campfire.

"Better grab some chow quick. It's going fast and it's a long ride home," the camp cook advised. As Bebe's buddy filled his plate and busily shook salt and pepper on his hot potatoes and fillets, the camp cook asked, "Well, did you enjoy your first Canadian trip?"

"Well, I'll tell you guys one thing," he responded as he took off his new hat. "I've known a lot of tough guys brave enough to get on the back of a Brahma bull or a bucking bronco. But I've never met anyone like you," he continued as he stretched out his arm and handed the Calgary Stampede hat to Moose Rider. "You deserve to wear a hat like this for riding that freaking moose yesterday."

Heads snapped up in unison like a herd of does reacting to the sound of a gunshot in the quiet woods.

"Well I'll be dipped!" exclaimed the cook.

"You mean to tell us you **really did** ride a moose?" shouted Gentleman Jim in amazement.

Moose Rider simply adjusted the Calgary Stampede hat on his head and poured hot coffee from the blackened pot.

Disbelief and amazement sent murmurs through the group. Bear shook his head in awe.

Meanwhile, Gentleman Jim scooped up the fillets that had fallen from his plate when he heard the news. "I suppose we gotta start calling you Moose Rider now."

"Moose Rider! Moose Rider!" whooped the Bear.

"I still don't believe you freakin' did that," remarked our Fearless Leader with some mixed emotion. "A guy's not gonna be able to top something like that."

Raising the metal coffee cup in a salute toward the lake, Moose Rider simply smiled and said, "Run, Dogie, Run." It was the only thing he could think of saying.

Tavern Tales

Throughout the picturesque North Country the ever-popular local tavern – or "tav-ern" to quote our Fearless Leader – is nothing less than an institution. It is a gathering place for the entire community throughout the year and **the** place to be during deer season.

Unless you're lucky enough to have grown up in the North County or have spent a lot of time in the region fishing or deer hunting, you may assume that we're talking about your basic bar or beer joint. No way! Nothing can be farther from the truth. I don't know how it happened that taverns have evolved into such significant community social structures, but that's the case in the wholesome little towns and sleepy villages scattered about the entire North Country.

Of course, taverns are the gathering places for celebrating the end of the work week like every other drinking establishment. Patrons gather to watch professional football games, participate in pool leagues and Halloween parties and flock to Saturday night dances featuring local bands of varying musical ability. Look closer, though, and you'll see that taverns serve as social centers, newsrooms, weather stations and sports reporting desks, including the essential Monday morning quarterback sessions. Although taverns are in their glory during deer season, they serve other community purposes.

Gracious hosts of monthly service club meetings, North Country taverns sponsor numerous special events like the annual Lion's Club pancake breakfast and fund raisers conducted for any number of good causes. Without question, it's the local tavern that's the hot spot for the traditional North Country favorite, the Friday night fish fry. This event is attended as religiously as church in most communities, more religiously in others!

By the way, these North Country backwoods taverns aren't just for singles or couples. They're family venues, and you soon learn the names of all the local kids. Indeed, if you stick around over the years, you can watch them grow up. Community leaders hope their kids will stay in the small towns after graduating from high school instead of migrating to the big cities, at least most of 'em. When they do leave, folks at the local watering hole will continue to ask about their careers and families with genuine interest.

"Are you **really** taking your kids along to a tavern?" asked some of our out-of-state guests with obvious amazement. In the North Country, the response is a definite "You betcha!" Your offspring will be known by everyone at the tavern and basically held accountable for their actions. That same dynamic works equally well for some of the kids' parents and that ain't all that bad. Can there be a better place for your kids to be given deserved recognition for their accomplishments than in public at the tavern? Word of their achievements will get around town in no time, believe me.

Additionally, if your kids go with you they'll get to know the community leaders and realize that if people like them can make it in life, so can they. Some of these folks, especially those who have been elected to public office, hold court daily or weekly at the local tavern. Want to know what your legislature is doing for you, or to you? Head to the nearby tavern.

Taverns are not restricted to the locals, either. You'll have the opportunity to meet lots of new people – namely tourists – and enjoy the best home-cooked food in the North Country. Some folks unofficially classify another North Country institution, the "Supper Club," simply as a tavern with a bigger menu. But please don't call either of them a beer joint. That's a derogatory term used – and used appropriately in my personal opinion – for drinking establishments outside of the North Country.

Recently, I visited a beer joint in my new midwestern neighborhood. Comparing it to a North Country tavern, I'd classify it as a place where seedy lounge lizards drink too much, smoke cigarettes excessively, get obnoxious and act stupid. They're not places to take your kids by any stretch of the imagination, unless you want them to observe those who have taken an early exit off the human evolutionary highway. There is much more to the North Country tavern than guzzling beer and raising hell all night.

Call them "coffee klatches" or just plain old gossip groups, assemblies of both men and women meet each and every morning at a tavern to "take" coffee – instead of drinking it – as if it were the essential elixir of life. Come to think of it, coffee is a Scandinavian elixir over which earthy folks judiciously discuss local news and weather, report on their business and, on occasion, examine everyone else's. Senior patrons have also been known to play cards feverishly during these morning sessions. The stakes are high – the losers have to pay for the morning doses of elixir.

These busy local institutions are also a place where important public notices are posted. It is widely understood that people will actually see them at the tavern. The same goes for notices for the annual Lion's Club smelt fry, VFW auction sale, and local residents' "for sale" or "lost and found" items. You want to spread the word? Head for the tavern where the moccasin telegraph operates well into the night.

You can even get the latest news of local sportsmen's hunting and fishing adventures to Canada, the Dakotas, or other distant destinations long before they arrive home. Someone in the tavern will know.

Taverns are the central hubs of activity in the small towns that are scattered throughout the heart of the North Country. They are multi-purpose establishments but, above all, taverns are an integral part of a deer-hunting experience. Places where lovers of the white-tailed deer assemble to gather, tell, and listen to ... tales from the North Country.

*Part II: Deer Huntin'
with our Fearless Leader*

Oh! That First Buck

The unmatched thrill of taking that first mighty buck can never be forgotten, although the experience may occur at any time in one's hunting career. Or not! For Old Moe had hunted with the Fearless Leader's gang in the North Country for over 20 years without even coming close to taking his first buck.

"That's because I always chase them over to you guys," he rationalizes as he seemingly attempts to convince others of his generosity. "It's a lot more fun to give some of you young guys a chance. I don't care whether I ever shoot one or not." Right!

At the other end of the spectrum are those novice hunters who at least get the opportunity for their first buck within minutes after beginning their inaugural adventure into the field. Go figure!

Many factors enter into the grand scheme of first buck success: preparation, skill, luck, amount of time spent scouting, luck, having access to productive hunting land. And, of course, luck.

Joining up with a group of veteran hunting partners, I felt confident after having hunted unsuccessfully on my own during my first few deer seasons. Like nomads led by the renowned Fearless Leader, they cross the North Country in search of white-tailed deer. Successful and knowledgeable, they had hunted the same environs for years. Though preferring the serenity of hunting alone from a tree stand, I eagerly accepted an invitation to accompany them in search of the ghostly denizens of the forest. I wanted to feel the thrill of taking that elusive first buck, and I was willing to endure the long, arduous and semi-organized deer drives through the North Country as payment for getting my buck.

One could speculate that the practice of driving deer is a hand-me-down from distant yesteryear. Clearly, there are buffalo jumps where Native Americans on horseback herded bison over cliffs or similar geological formations. Nevertheless, I suspect that the first deer drives were conducted on foot much like the pursuit we were about to commence.

I watched in awe as our Fearless Leader predicted which gully an escaping buck would take. He directed the operation from his pickup with advice from the usual cast of characters. Before each drive, a basic plan is devised that is based upon the number of standers and drivers available and their respective skills, or lack thereof. Every hunter is assigned specific responsibilities. Loosely translated, it appeared to me that the old timers, along with at least three or four other hunters who had driven the preceding two or three drives, would always stand. Standers were given specific locations that were known escape routes. It was hoped these positions would enable them to ambush an unwary buck.

I was dropped off at a small, triangular wooded section comprised of a point of land that led toward a mirror-image point extending from an adjoining woods. I had doubts that any buck would be dumb enough to cross the open space between the points. But if he did, it made sense that he would move toward my location on the west point since it would offer him the path of least exposure that deer, especially those big old secretive bucks, prefer.

Once in place, I surveyed my surroundings. Snow covered the landscape on the mostly clear morning, and the wind was nearly undetectable. While the crusty snow was not deep enough to satisfy local sled dog enthusiasts, it covered the ground completely. Gazing across my point of land to the other side that sloped gently downhill, I identified numerous weed species poking through the snow. Somehow the scene, though not as colorful, reminded me of a picture of prairie grasses in an old *National Geographic*. I liked the looks of it – liked it a lot.

I stood behind several black spruce trees to break my body's outline. Old Indian trick. I planned to remain motionless, knowing that whitetails may not have the best eyesight when they are at close range, but that they can detect the slightest movement like a soaring bald eagle. I wondered if my hunting companions were concealed or standing in the open. I glanced in both directions.

On my left was a 14-year-old hunter with a .30-.30, and to the south stood the irascible "Wild Man," whose brother I had come to know well on several memorable South Dakota pheasant hunts. We waited.

Standard procedure dictates that once the standers and drivers are deposited at their starting spots and the vehicles parked, a signal is given then passed down the line from hunter to hunter. The troops march into the woods in a theoretically unified formation. Realistically, the young and highly charged younger drivers race through the woods. Alder thickets and other obstacles slow some drivers; others don't follow their compasses as they should. The end result is that no two drives are the same, but the woods are disturbed enough to rattle most of the deer. Of course, cagey old bucks make a practice of easily and silently slipping around even the most experienced hunters.

Later, I would experience the whitetail's uncanny ability to sneak by me even though I had hunted, watched and photographed deer for years and could spot them pretty darned well.

Standing in a hardwood forest with vegetation of mixed age and moderate density, I knew deer were heading my way. One of the approaching drivers could clearly see both me and the deer and shouted, "Get ready; they're coming right for you." Staring intently, I could not see any deer and was amazed when the driver repeated his warning. The deer somehow detected me and used a very slight depression not 75 yards away to keep out of my sight. Not a couple deer – but about 20 – sneaked past. I finally saw them only after hearing their hooves when they crossed the road behind me. Is it any wonder that whitetails have been so successful and that they can stir our emotions and imagination like no other animal?

No one knows for sure what it takes to satisfy the deer gods so that they decide to reward a hunter, or precisely when the amount of down payment has met the required threshold. Maybe it was a case of dumb luck, but the deer gods smiled upon my point of real estate in the North Country that day. For loping gracefully and elegantly in the morning stillness came a beautiful doe. Lifting her legs daintily and deliberately, she leaped like a young, confident ballerina. And in hot pursuit came a tremendous buck sporting polished antlers backlit by the morning sun. Those antlers completely filled the forest – or so it seemed. There were tines everywhere. Lofty and majestic. Bobbing up and down and headed in my direction. Surely they would pass within 30 yards. My heart raced.

Like a super computer without input data to crunch, my thought processes crashed. Desire erased logic and sound advice. I wanted my first buck. Desperately. I froze.

As the duo loped in their synchronized North Country ballet, I waited for them to get closer, but the young hunter to my left spied them. I watched in horror as he shouldered and hastily fired his .30-.30. I can still hear the sound of his shot as it echoed in the forest. The blast shattered the silence and my heart at the same time. The deer stopped suddenly – which raised my anxiety to new heights – then turned toward the direction of the shot.

I thought to myself that it could not be happening. I wanted to shout "NO! That's my buck." My first opportunity at a buck. My first wall-hanging trophy. Hadn't I paid my dues over the years? To my amazement and relief, the stately pair bounded onward unscathed. Puffs of steam billowed from their moist nostrils into the frosty morning air. Growing larger and nobler with each stride as they came within range, they followed the south side of my point of land and moved away from the young hunter's field of view. My opportunity had finally arrived. That glorious chance for my first buck.

My breathing stopped, and I tensed. Wait now – two more seconds – but don't let him get by you. Pounding like a pile driver, my heart pumped rich adrenaline into my system, and light-headedness overwhelmed me.

Raising my new ought-six with lead-weighted arms – I led the bounding buck and squeezed off a shot. Seemingly oblivious to the danger, the pair continued unharmed. As they neared another opening in the trees to my right, I fought to gather my wits and breath. I swallowed hard and sucked in air. Struggling to think logically and to overcome the dreaded grasp of buck fever, I experienced all of its symptoms within three or four heartbeats. Somehow, I remembered that I did not have to lead with a high-powered rifle as I did when hunting South Dakota pheasants. As the multi-tined buck passed the opening in the black spruce – though my hands were trembling – I pulled the trigger again. The buck responded by immediately dropping to the snowy earth. I gasped for a breath. I wanted to run to him and drop on my knees and embrace him. Filled with joy, I wanted to shout but I couldn't. Instead, I began to grin.

The young hunter, obviously hopeful that his lone shot had brought down the heavy brute, ran across the open area. "I'm pretty sure I got him!" shouted the .30-.30 owner. "My gun jammed after the first shot, but I think I got him. See how many times he was hit."

It was easy to ascertain that a lone, strategic or lucky shot had brought the stately buck down, and I continued to experience the emotions that must have existed since those first deer drives were made by the ancient peoples of the land. Feelings of honor, joy, respect, awe and perhaps a little sadness, mingled as I contemplated having ended the life of a princely animal. He was my buck. My first buck. And I stood in the small point of woods that North Country morning and grinned uncontrollably.

Word spread quickly down the line since the drive had concluded. "We got a buck down!"

"Who got it?" demanded the Fearless Leader from a distance. He kept close track of his troops and their successes and failures.

"Doc! A 10 pointer," responded Wild Man from my right.

"Oh my God-frey!" exclaimed Jackson as he spied the fallen buck – then forwarded the news farther down the line of hunters. "Hey! Doc got a 10 pointer! His first buck!"

Gathering around the prized buck, the troops examined the antlers, guessed its weight, and admired the beautiful creature. Jackson said, "You got yourself a wall-mounter, Doctor." I still wore my childish grin.

"You shot it, you gut it," commanded the already impatient Wild Man. "Let's get it over with so we can make another drive. You're gonna hold us up."

As I readied my sharp, gleaming Buck knife, I was glad I had watched a video describing the correct evisceration procedure. Smelling the viscera was a new experience, and the blade passed easily through the right tissues, though my hands were unsteady. I remember it well.

But most of all, I remember the other hunters gathering around and admiring my first buck as they offered congratulations. I still vividly remember the Fearless Leader's old man saying, "I've got to give the Doc a pat on the back." Proud and humbled, I washed my hands with snow and stood up feeling like a true member of the gathered band of North Country hunters. My knees were still weak. I couldn't stop grinning.

Grabbing an antler at its base, two of my fellow hunters ceremoniously dragged my prized buck to the Fearless Leader's pickup and hoisted it into the truck bed. Someone grabbed a broken branch and propped open the buck's chest cavity. It would weigh 195 pounds after being field dressed.

Though I dutifully continued the hunt, my mind was locked on my prized buck. Throughout the long afternoon I glanced back – or stared back – through the pickup window and admired my first buck. I felt proud. The Fearless Leader was proud, too. He left the tailgate down and watched for the reaction of other hunters when they saw the trophy. When we returned from the DNR check station, the Fearless Leader parked his truck directly in front of his "tav-ern" next to the highway so everyone could see my first buck.

Finally it had happened. My turn had come to buy that special one-time round of drinks at the tavern. The round was accompanied by more congratulatory proclamations.

I couldn't wait until someone asked me, "Did you get your deer?" I looked forward to strolling into the corporate coffee shop where co-workers gathered to pass judgement on the season's successes. I couldn't wait to get the mount back from the taxidermist after an excruciatingly long wait. And I couldn't wait to hunt the spot henceforth known as "Doc's 10-Point Drive" again.

But I would not have to wait any longer for that one monumental event. For there is only one heartfelt experience of taking that first buck. And it is sweet!

Which Way Does
Your Compass Point?

Every time the Fearless Leader lined us up to begin a new drive during deer season, I checked to make sure that my compass was clipped securely to my blaze-orange hunting jacket and in plain sight. What could be worse than the prospect of getting lost in the middle of a deer drive and having to face the disdain and torment of the hunting party afterward?

We were a diverse troop, an interesting mix of guys and gals. A melting pot of ethnic backgrounds and religions, although such characteristics mean nothing during deer camp. It occurred to me that the Fearless Leader tried to be fair and patient with everyone. Unless, of course, we did something that was incredibly stupid – which happened often enough.

While a couple of the older guys seldom took a shot at a deer, he didn't belittle them. Actually, he made sure that they received a fair share of venison at season's end to help feed their families through the long and harsh North Country winter. One of the advantages of party hunting is the opportunity for good hunters, like our distinguished guide, to help out others by shooting more than one deer. He loved doing just that – especially big bucks.

Hunting as a party also brought the group together. We experienced good times as well as events that we would rather forget. Call it "bonding," if you must. Perhaps hunting as a group fulfills some sort of deep-rooted urge or instinct that increases the odds of a species to survive. Maybe we were just sharing the joy of what we all had in common, hunting the magnificent whitetail. Whatever it was, it bound us together as a hunting outfit, and we were very successful.

Because we possessed a reputation as one of the best hunting parties in the region, our Fearless Leader was often besieged with requests from others to hunt with us for a day or two. Some of the requests granted were not popular with the troops.

"Transient hunters," scoffed Avis, "I wish he wouldn't invite those guys like that. Most of 'em never show up again to help with the drives if they do get a buck. Doc, it ain't right."

Avis was right. The previous deer season, one of our Commander's buddies from Milwaukee bagged a stately hardwood buck, then promptly loaded up and headed for home. Had it not been for him, the mossy antlered buck may have continued on a rut route trail leading to my position near the edge of the hardwoods. It would have been my largest buck ever. Count that as one of my memorable events with transient deer hunters.

Another episode the following year left an indelible mark on my memory. Now here is the way I remember it, and I can tell you that I recall the event as if it happened last week. It really did happen this way:

He wasn't the sort of guy that you or I would pick for a party hunt. Short and cocky, he was an arrogant young man in his late twenties. Already divorced, he considered himself worldly and bragged of his exploits in the woods and in bed. His long wavy hair reminded me of a television evangelist, and he bore a sinister, reptilian smile. Carrying an old, unkempt deer rifle seemed inconsistent with the new orange coveralls that he was wearing. His 12-inch rubber boots appeared out of place as well. Why had the Fearless Leader invited him? Maybe he owed him a favor, or perhaps the Fearless Leader sensed that nobody else would ask him to hunt, and he felt sorry for him. I do not know – I don't second-guess our Fearless Leader.

Avis, a stocky ex-marine with bushy eyebrows and a graying flattop, mumbled something derogatory about the rubber boots, and I could tell that the seasoned veteran was not pleased with our new companion. Who had, by the way, shown up 20 minutes late and then needed to buy ammunition at the sport shop, followed by a stop at the tavern for coffee and a sandwich to take along for lunch. Emerging from the tavern, he paused on the sidewalk to flirt with an attractive passerby.

"Are we going to go shoot a deer today or are we going to stand around and shoot the breeze?" complained Avis. Although he didn't say "breeze."

"What's your hurry?" responded the newcomer. "I'll probably have my buck while the rest of you chumps are trying to figure out how to load your guns."

Inaudible and possibly unrepeatable words came out of Avis's mouth as he turned and headed toward his rust-infested white and yellow GMC with squeaky brakes. He affectionately called the truck "Betsy."

"Come on, Doc," I heard Avis say as he glanced over his right shoulder at the newcomer. "You're going with me. The banty rooster is riding with the Fearless Leader if he's gonna be huntin' at all." We were off to a rocky start.

Once the troops were assembled and order was restored by the Fearless Leader, he led us on the first drive, known as the "Sandpit Drive." Each drive was assigned – or earned – its own name in the North Country. Wild Man downed a spike buck half way through Sandpit while letting off only four shots from his .30-30. Perhaps a new personal record for him! Nobody else saw anything, and we were all eager to get on to the next drive.

"We're making the Pump Handle Drive next," declared our

Commander-in-Chief. There were a few groans. Believe me, the Pump Handle is a real swamp! Mild temperatures and above-normal snowfall meant slow travelling and perhaps wet feet when breaking through patches of ice. But the thick cover of the swamp was also a haven for big bucks when the lead started flying during November in the North Country.

Dividing up the troops between drivers and standers, the Fearless Leader gave us special instructions for the tricky swamp maneuver. We listened carefully. Most of us, that is.

"Make sure you drivers head due north and keep your eyes open for the tracks of the standers in the snow. If you see human tracks going in, don't cross them. Just come on out, even if you aren't sure if you've gone the quarter-mile to where the trail runs through. Because if you miss it, you could go on for two miles since there aren't any other roads through there, so pay attention."

"Aye, Aye Sir!" mocked the new guy. "Can we go kill something now?"

"I wanna make sure everyone's ready. This one's a bitch," said our Captain with a hint of concern and agitation in his voice. "You got a compass on you?" he asked the mouthy transient as he visually scanned the new coveralls. He liked to make sure everyone was well prepared, especially for the Pump Handle.

"No, but I don't

need a stupid compass," he replied with a lizard-like smirk. "I can walk in a straight line. Can't you?" He looked around to see who had enjoyed his humor. No one had.

"Better take this extra one of mine. If you get turned around you'll be in there for hours and cut into our huntin' time. You'll need to take a lot of detours around the tag alders and stands of black spruce. Be careful not to go too far to the left, or you'll get wet," warned our leader. "There's a lot of sphagnum out that direction."

"What a bunch a wimps," remarked the transient as the insistent Fearless Leader pinned the compass on him. It was like a teacher pinning a note on an unruly schoolboy. "I thought you chumps were taking me on a deer hunt, not a Cub Scout outing. Let's go!"

"All right folks, load 'em up and let's hit it," commanded our leader when he finished the difficult task of organizing the drive. His patience was being tried to the limit. "Remember, keep it due north and don't forget to come out if you see tracks." Showtime at the Pump Handle – we were underway.

Swamp hunting is demanding. I remember trying to avoid large expanses of ice by stepping on elevated clumps of dead grasses while watching for deer, deer tracks, hunter tracks and also trying to judge the distance to the trail. Busting through occasional thin sheets of ice made glass-shattering sounds that likely would stampede any deer into the next county, instead of driving them toward the standers. No buck in its right mind would try to circle back behind such commotion.

Dense stands of leather leaf and Labrador tea, both growing nearly three feet tall, seemed to grope at my legs and drive me off course. Mats of bog rosemary snagged the toes of my boots as I pushed through the Pump Handle. I also managed to pick up a couple scratches on my face from briars, and my clothing was transporting seeds from all sorts of unidentified swamp vegetation. Glancing at my compass frequently gave me a false sense of security, and I kept repeating the Fearless Leader's instructions to myself. Maybe I was wimpy in terms of finding my way through the Pump Handle. Well, so be it.

Although I didn't see any deer or hear any shots, I did manage to identify the trail left by the standers on their way in. I waited there for the other drivers to come out.

"See anything?" asked Wild Man, who showed up first. He belched loudly.

"Zippo!" I replied, eyeing his right pant leg that was much darker up to his knee than the left.

"Got a little damp in one spot," he said while shaking his leg. "That drive gets tougher every year. Look! Here comes Avis."

"Driving deer through there is kinda like trying to herd cats," said Avis, who had either broken through the ice or wet his pants in the excitement. He was breathing hard and droplets of perspiration beaded his forehead. "See anything boys?"

"Nothing here, Avis. Were you the last guy in the line?" I asked.

"I think your buddy, the jerk, was between me and Wild Man," replied Avis as he looked to Wild Man for affirmation. "He either went too fast and walked on out, or he's still out there picking daisies somewhere. Let's go on out. I ain't waitin' for him."

Heading toward the road, we met the standers and remaining drivers along the way, and then gathered around the Fearless Leader's pickup for some well-deserved coffee. He winced when he learned that the new guy was missing.

"He should be along pretty soon," he speculated. "He couldn't get lost 'cause I gave him a compass." He then quickly changed the subject and started planning the next drive we would take, assuming we recovered from the Pump Handle. The coffee continued to flow.

"Get out the maps!" demanded the Fearless Leader a half hour and numerous complaints later. "Let's try to figure out where he could have gone if he missed the trail."

"That's easy," remarked Avis. "He could be somewhere between here and Outer Mongolia. Do you wanna go lookin' for him?" He was getting testy and the Fearless Leader knew it, but he understood Avis and didn't comment.

"More than likely he would have to cross the Mehoff Road," added Wild Man as he wiped his nose on his sleeve. "Assumin' that he went straight, of course."

"He would have to!" responded our leader. "Unless he lost my compass, he'll come out there all right. I told him not to cross any human tracks without coming out. Why don't you head over there, Wild Man, and we'll stay here? And keep your CB on." Normally he would have asked Avis to go since he could be relied upon without reservation, but he was sensitive to Avis's growing impatience and irritation.

"Let's go sit in Betsy and have a sandwich, Doc. Ain't nothin' else we can do for now," remarked Avis, taking another shot at the missing transient. That sounded good to me. Everyone else drifted toward their waiting vehicles and ate, smoked or napped. Stillness returned to the swamp. A raven croaked far off in the distance, and the sky darkened.

Big snowflakes falling from the sky added to the tension of the situation. Tracks in the snow could be covered in a matter of a few minutes. Time was passing, and we could be hunting.

"By God there he is!" exclaimed Avis, expelling chocolate chip cookie crumbs from his mouth and pointing toward the lost hunter. The cookie crumbs danced erratically across Betsy's dashboard.

What a sight he was! His brand new coveralls were wet and completely black clear up to his waist. His evangelistic hair was soaked with perspiration. Looking like a cross between a drowned rat and the Creature from the Black Lagoon, he cradled his gun in his arms. Stopping, and then stooping, he glanced to his right as if he had seen something moving in the swamp.

Continuing on, he walked toward us in a nonchalant manner as if the last hour and 15 minutes had been a normal part of the swamp drive.

"How many bucks did you get out there, Daniel Boone?" Avis shouted out of Betsy's window, showing the first signs of emotion other than irritation. He was tickled. "Hee hee! Look at that dumb shit will you, Doc?"

Leaping out of the truck, the Fearless Leader joined in, "How the hell did you get lost?" he questioned. He had become somewhat agitated, which was uncharacteristic of him. "Just where in the heck have you been?"

Ignoring the acid remarks, the lost hunter was unfazed by the disgusted looks of the others. His rubber boots made sloshing sounds with each step.

"I wasn't lost," he boasted. "I kinda knew where I was all the time, or at least most of the time, but I definitely wasn't lost," smirked lizard lips. "If I had my own compass, I would have been here sooner. But that dumb compass you loaned me … it ain't worth a damn."

"So what the heck can go wrong with a compass?" hooted our ordained leader.

The new guy unclipped the Fearless Leader's compass from the pathetic coveralls and tossed it to him as he responded with sarcasm. "It doesn't work right. Which the hell way does your stupid compass point anyway?"

Oh, that Fearless Leader! He always had a magical way of bringing the troops back together at the opportune time, even the touchy Avis. He did it again that day as we gathered at the end of the Pump Handle Drive. He united us in fits of laughter and consummated another North Country tale when he replied, "I don't know what kind of fancy compass you have or where you got it, Einstein, but I think you'll find that around here, all of the compasses point toward the North!"

Guts and Glory

Venison pepperoni is an epicurean delight when accompanied with a thick slice of Wisconsin cheese and a cold Milwaukee beer. But it was all gone! So were the delicate venison chops and smoked summer sausages! And the scrumptious venison jerky had been gobbled down within days of leaving the smokehouse. Fortunately, deer season had returned to the North Country, and we hastened into our treasured woods during opening weekend in search of fresh meat.

"I can smell the inside of Jim's Meat Market right now!" I said to the Fearless Leader. "Man, what I wouldn't give for a big stick of Jim's smoked pepperoni. We gotta get some fresh meat today."

"I'm not concerned about 'pecker-oni' right now." A case of beer is the only thing on my mind," answered the Great One, his forehead deeply furrowed and a slight hint of concern in his voice. He was in danger of losing the traditional opening weekend wager with Moose Rider. Now losing a case of beer, when compared to the income from the brisk carryout and tavern business during "orange week," doesn't sound like much of a loss. But one doesn't have to go beyond Rocket Science 101 to conclude that it's not about the money or beer; it's about reputation, pride and ego. And the Fearless Leader was in a predicament … again.

The social order of some deer hunters – I have concluded – is exactly like that of the big white-tailed bucks they pursue with passion. Both coexist harmoniously during most of the year. It is at the time of the rut – which coincides with deer season – that the competition starts for real. It is a time to test one's prowess. A time to challenge the other dominant bucks for supremacy. A time to strive to win some money on the big buck board. Our Fearless Leader's goal was to claim the ultimate wager placed on the traditional big buck challenge, namely a case of cold brewskies.

In spite of the DNR's rosy predictions of a record deer harvest, another in a long string of unproductive openers was underway. Where were all of those bonus deer? Wasn't the Fearless Leader's hunting party the best in all of the North Country? I was not overly confident that I'd take a buck, but I knew the Fearless Leader would come through for us. He would bring home some venison before the hunt was over. He always brought the meat home. You could bet on that. A lot!

The initial half of opening weekend had been biting cold and meatless. Now Sunday's wimpy sun had nearly completed its low arc across the blue November sky. Gray shadows of the bare white birch and poplars were growing longer and darker on the crusty snow. Dead leaves lay scattered on the snow's cold surface, and numerous footprints were visible where deer had traveled a couple days before.

"Deer track soup isn't going to taste too good tonight," said the Fearless Leader with disappointment. "I'm afraid Moose Rider may have me beat." The legendary dimples were absent, and we only had about three hours remaining to bring home the brewskies. There was still hope.

Abandoning our fruitless deer drive strategy on Sunday

afternoon, we separated from the rest of the party. Our leader and I rode in his pickup, a.k.a. the "meat wagon," to the local paper company's land. It was a huge tract of real estate, half of which had been clear-cut three years previously. Crisscrossed deer tracks were present on the back edge of the property where we had experienced some memorable autumn grouse hunting. Leading to the safety of the adjacent swamp were three rut route trails, which we had earlier recorded on our topo maps. We hoped to spot a quality buck at the far side of the clear cut. If we could see one, the Fearless Leader could bring him down skillfully.

Approaching a small clearing, which provides just enough space for a pickup to park and which offers an expansive view of the clear-cut, we uncased our binoculars. As the truck came to a halt, I climbed out searching for the best vantage point. At the same instant, as if on cue, a concealed buck burst from dense cover across the clearing. Making a fatal mistake, he bounded directly toward us.

"Get your gun! Get your gun!" I blurted out, trying not to shout or panic.

The Fearless Leader's face displayed a puzzled look. He was still in the truck studying the map, and he hadn't seen the buck coming in our direction. But he uncased his trusty Remington as fast as he could and jumped out of the vehicle. He reacts in a hurry when under pressure.

It was unreal! The antlered trophy continued gracefully leaping straight toward us, antler tines flashing in the waning sun just like the stories written in the popular sporting magazines. What an awesome sight!

Instantly the sound of gunfire filled the quiet clear-cut. But it wasn't the Fearless Leader's gun that shattered the silence. Standing in an illegal permanent deer stand constructed of several whole sheets of plywood, a slob hunter was blazing away at the buck. Bang! Bang! Bang! Or maybe it was Ka-bang! Ka-bang!

Ka-bang! I'm not sure. Doesn't matter. The third slug from the goon's 12-gauge sent the marvelous creature into a steep nose-dive in the snow. The 10 pointer didn't move again.

Standing there with our mouths open, we watched the whole scene in awe. We were like two kids in the old days staring wide-eyed at a shoot 'em up western during a Saturday matinee. A slob hunter had shot the Fearless Leader's winning buck (and our pepperoni factory) right out from under our noses! Is there no justice in the North Country?

Climbing down from his apartment-sized tree stand, the bovine hunter grunted like a caribou as he shuffled over to the crime scene. His orange parka could not enclose the big stomach that bounced like a huge blob of JELL-O. Two of his fellow pillagers soon appeared from nowhere, and they huddled together over the fallen buck like a pride of lions over a fresh kill.

Marching over to them, the incensed Fearless Leader raised the issue of the illegal stand. But the slob mob denied any knowledge of its construction as they gutted the foolish buck and dragged him away posthaste.

Our senses were numb and our spirits plummeted. Trooping back through the crunchy snow, we returned to the empty meat wagon. The CB radio was crackling when we climbed aboard. My hunting partner reached down and turned it off after a few moments. I could tell that he didn't want to talk. Silence once again overtook the clear-cut, and the blue sky continued to fade to purple and clouded over with a thin layer of stratus clouds.

"What'll we do now?" I asked, pouring a cup of hot chocolate and hoping to end the uncomfortable quiet spell. All I could think about was driving to Jim's Meat Market on Monday morning and savoring the aromatic smell of freshly smoked pepperoni. We were in desperate need of a miracle. He had made them happen before!

"I'm not in much of a hurry to go back to the tav-ern to see Moose Rider. He's won the beer this opener. I got him last year, though, with a little help from a bungee cord and those antlers you've got in your shed," he said as he managed a weak smile. "That was a real buck caper all right."

"No big deal. There's always next year, and I still might get a big one before the seasons over," he said in a low disappointed voice while his tired eyes remained fixed on the clear-cut.

Twenty more minutes of uncomfortable silence passed. I could tell he was searching for an alternative plan. He could always come up with the perfect solution when the pressure mounted. A few more minutes passed. Then, shaking his head, he issued a long and deliberate sigh. He opened the squeaky door and got out of the truck.

"Wait here, Doc," he said in a raspy voice as he pitched his hunting gloves and cap on the truck's dashboard. Walking stiff legged he returned to the scene of the calamity in the clear-cut and paused by the viscera that were still steaming in the fading purple light. He glanced from side to side.

When immortals fail, it leaves a lasting impression on those who admire them. I was crushed when my Yankees lost the World Series. I remember fighting back the tears as a youngster when my Indy 500 racing hero was killed at the Speedway. But the event that had the greatest impact on me was that day in the clear-cut when the revered Fearless Leader took out his hunting knife and stooped down on his knees. My white-tail mentor and buck-hunting hero, the Buckslayer Emeritus of the North Country, harvested our only fresh meat of opening weekend ... by robbing the heart and liver from the abandoned gut pile!

The Cutting Edge

He was about to make one of the most important decisions a deer hunter can make. Such decisions aren't made without careful and thorough deliberation.

"Can't you at least give me your personal opinion?" he begged the Fearless Leader.

"You're the only one who can make that decision, Robbie, my man," was the reply.

Survival could depend upon one's selection of a hunting knife, although probably not in his case. Standing and admiring every single one of the weapons, he was like ... well, like a grown man in a sporting goods store. Some knives were arranged in boxes with individual compartments and some were strung up and enclosed in special glass cases that rotated when a knob was turned on top of the case. Back and forth his eyes roamed over shining beauties with names such as *Buck Knives*, *Uncle Henry*, and the venerable *Old Timer*. Searching for a hunting knife that looked and felt good, he didn't know anything about brand names and, furthermore, couldn't care less. He wanted the perfect-feeling classical deer-hunting knife.

Like all of the rest of us inspired deer hunters, he didn't get out in the field nearly as much as he wanted.

"I'm all covered up at the office," he would always say.

Actually, come to think of it, he seemed to get away from his insurance office much easier to play golf during the warm days of summer. But that is neither here nor there. Deer season was approaching, and his large, well-dressed frame was bent over the glass counter of the Fearless Leader's sport shop.

Gregarious and well liked, he had moved to the North Country from the big city only a few years back. Lacking in outdoor skills, or perhaps just taking advantage of a good thing, he relied upon the locals to let him know when fish were biting or to help him prepare for hunting season. Assistance was eagerly offered, although it was often accompanied by a little mischief to help introduce the gullible city boy to the customs and traditions of the great North Country. It was always a treat to take him into the field.

Our Fearless Leader helped introduce him to the ways of the white-tailed deer. While hiking one morning late that summer to show him the local cranberry bog, the Fearless Leader came across some deer droppings. Pointing out the difference in size of the "deer poop," he described the relationship between their characteristics and the size and sex of whitetails.

"Those babies look like black jelly beans," said Robbie as he eyed the small, shining black pellets of a fawn.

You can bet that our Fearless Leader was prepared. Holding a couple of the pellets in his left hand, he told Robbie that he could tell the sex of the deer by tasting the pellets. Popping a couple of pellets into his mouth our Fearless Leader confidently stated, "Yep! This one is a doe; tastes a little sweeter than buck pellets."

"Yuck! That's disgusting!" shouted Robbie. "You must be freakin' crazy, man!"

Maintaining his composure, our Fearless Leader told him it was an old lesson taught to him, and he would be delighted to teach Robbie the technique. Back in the confines of the enclosed pickup it didn't take Robbie long to get the scent of licorice jelly beans. Then he realized that the Fearless Leader had held the deer droppings in his left hand and popped some of the black jelly beans into his mouth using his right hand. He loved it!

"That's a good one, you crazy son-of-a-gun," blurted Robbie. "I'm gonna have to play that one on some of my insurance buddies."

Robbie's insurance business was doing well compared to other local agents. Given the local practice of referring to everyone by a nickname and given the seemingly universal attitude toward insurance agents, Robbie was often affectionately referred to as "Rob-me" by local deer hunters.

He had large brown eyes that were soft, yet attentive, and his piercing stare was like that of an alert doe. However, his most striking feature was his laugh. Well, it wasn't really a laugh. His laugh and his high-pitched, raspy voice were co-mingled. Expressing something, especially with emotion, could be either described as laughing or talking, because he choked them both out together. Everyone in town found the sound pleasing to the ear.

A couple seasons back he decided to hunt deer for the first time. He didn't have time to prepare, of course, so two members of the Fearless Leader's hunting party agreed to build a tree stand for him in an area where they have hunted for over a dozen years. Having had everything prepared for him, on opening morning Robbie marched with them through a black spruce swamp and into a remote area on the north side of Wisconsin's Little Brule River just west of Highway P. Halfway back to their stands they paused to catch their breath beneath an osprey nesting platform erected by the DNR. Now Robbie had never heard of artificial nesting platforms. Perched on the very top of the trunk of a weathered 60-foot spruce was the simple square platform.

"What the hell is that?" asked Robbie as he eyed the platform with surprise.

"That's it!" one of the guides quickly remarked as he pointed to the platform on its precarious perch. "That's the tree stand we put up for you, ol' buddy."

Robbie stared at the tiny square and studied the tree from top to bottom. Then he fixed his eyes on the guide, and in his jovial voice-laugh, blurted out in all seriousness, "You've gotta be shitin' me, man. I'd never make it all the way up there." Only after the guys were doubled over in laughter did he realize they were joking.

Although a no-nonsense kind of businessman, he appreciated a good joke, even if it was on him. Being a good sport often meant that one would try to figure out a good trick to pull on Robbie just to hear the sound of that wonderful, infectious voice-laugh.

Back at the knife counter, neither jokes nor laughter were on Robbie's mind as he deliberated over which knife he would carry on his hip into the woods. After handling each one carefully and spending nearly two hours at the task, he made his final selection. Elated over his purchase, he headed for the Fearless Leader's tavern to celebrate his decision with a beer or three. He liked his beer and he liked visiting the tavern since many of his customers (and potential customers) wandered in and out of the local landmark.

Resting on the wooden barstool, he turned and rotated the new knife in his office-protected hands. A warm smile came to his face. Admiring the feel of the handle, he took satisfaction in the way light flashed off of the gleaming blade like a tiny airport beacon on a dark night. Closing the blade, he inserted his new lethal weapon into its black leather case then reopened it again and tested the sharpness of the blade against his index finger. He was delighted with the results of his monumental decision.

Entering the tavern, Gray Sky, one of his osprey platform guides, shuffled over and took the stool next to Robbie. He urged the stool toward the bar as its legs protested the move with a loud squeal.

"Whatcha up to, Rob-me?" queried the guide as he watched the bartender's movements for an opportunity to catch his eye.

"Just sittin' here admiring my new knife," was Robbie's reply as he continued to fondle his newly acquired treasure.

"Nice lookin' toadsticker you got there, Rob-me. Is that an *Old Timer*?" inquired Gray Sky as he eyed the knife in Robbie's hands.

Bolting upright as if zapped by lightning, Robbie looked at his companion with an expression of disbelief written on his face. The piercing brown eyes were wide, and he uttered something that resembled a gasp. His eyes moved to the knife and back again at the man next to him.

"What?" asked his friend, startled by Robbie's sudden reaction. "What?"

"Hell, no! It's not an old timer," blurted the indignant Robbie. "How could it be an old timer? I told you I just **bought** the son-of-a-bitch!"

Deer Defense Mechanisms

Every serious observer of wild deer has heard that eerie sound, and even the most experienced deer hunter can be startled by the sudden strange noise. Although our Fearless Leader could not remember the first time he had heard the explosive sound of a deer's alarm snort, he would never forget Rob-me's first encounter last October.

Fall had descended on the North Country, and its beauty motivated many to abandon their normal responsibility or irresponsibility, as the case may be, and head for the colorful outdoors. Stunning golds, reds and yellows painted the trees and began to carpet the forest floor. Fall in the North Country means frosty mornings, ruffed grouse and whitetails.

"I've got to get out of this office. It's too darn nice outside," Rob-me had said. "Let's go put up a deer stand or go scouting some new territory, anything instead of wasting this great fall day sitting on my butt in the office. I can jump into a pair of jeans and ditch my suit here at the office."

He is seldom seen in jeans. He is the best-dressed person in town and also maintains the nicest yard of anyone. It looks like the fairways at the nearby country club where he is an active member. His business contacts and country club connections help him to be one of the most effective spokespersons during our annual spring visit to our legislators in Madison. But it was fall, and deer season was not far off.

"Be there in 10 minutes," responded the Fearless Leader. He didn't need much of an excuse to drop his numerous business duties and head for the woods. He was always ready when deer were involved.

"What do you want me to bring?" asked Rob-me. "Any equipment or tools to work on a deer huntin' stand?"

"Nothing except a jacket since it might get a little nippy if we're out in the woods for a long time," the Fearless Leader advised him.

"Well, just get over here before the blasted phone rings again. I think I'd like to do some serious scouting," said the insurance agent, promptly hanging up the phone without waiting for a reply.

With bow-hunting season approaching, Rob-me had gotten the hunting bug along with most of the other celebrated members of the Fearless Leader's party. Although he really didn't know how to go about scouting, he liked the adventurous sound of the word. Indeed, he was hooked on the idea of a fall bow hunt, and he was seriously engaged in doing his homework.

Now Rob-me was a good student of the magnificent white-tail and learned a great number of interesting facts about the popular animal. After reading *Whitetail Country* and admiring the photography of Daniel J. Cox, he was raring to take his new-found knowledge into the field. He learned that deer rub their foreheads and antlers on trees and other available stationary objects and they deposit a pheromone scent from the glands near their eyes – the preorbital glands. He had also learned that bucks dig out circular areas with their hooves called "scrapes." Then they urinate over tarsal glands located on the inside of their back legs to deposit scent onto the scrape. Like a schoolboy eager to impress others, Rob-me brought up the subject of deer behavior at every available opportunity.

When the Fearless Leader showed up in front of the insurance office a few minutes later in his veteran pickup truck, Rob-me hopped in and immediately began discussing facts about deer behavior.

"I think its neat how bucks mark their territories by rubbing their scent on trees and stuff and that lets others know that this area is already taken. Kinda like a 'no trespassing' sign without words. Pretty doggoned neat!"

"Neat, all right," remarked the Fearless Leader who had known that fact since he was about eight years old. "Neat!" he repeated as he put the truck in gear and eased out of the driveway.

"Can you believe it? Those bucks pee down their back leg to deposit their scent on a scrape to leave messages," continued Rob-me, chuckling at the thought. "And once you find a scrape, there's usually an overhanging limb that's been rubbed and licked by the buck. Tells other deer somethin' about him, too."

"Sounds like you're getting to be quite the deer biologist," the Fearless Leader teased. He enjoyed tweaking the affable insurance agent.

"And get this; I just learned that deer have this pad thing in the top of their mouth. Those suckers don't have any upper front teeth!"

"Sounds like a couple redneck huntin' buddies of mine," joked our leader as they drove on toward the woods.

When they reached their destination at the end of the gravel road, they parked the truck and went off into the woods like a couple of 10-year-olds laughing and enjoying each other's company and the allure of the outdoors. They checked the integrity of an old tree stand the Fearless Leader had constructed several years previously and set off to check on one of the new stands erected for the insurance man. The site was called the "tanglewood stand" because of the dense alders and briars. The Fearless Leader suggested sneaking in as quietly as possible since the site had experienced little human encroachment. Advancing quietly, which may have been a first for these two mischievous characters; they were in sight of the stand when a sudden and intense "Wuusssshhhuu!" sounded. A plump doe catapulted from cover a mere 30 feet away and literally crashed through the dry vegetation. Out of the cover and up the ridge she went along with her two spotted fawns. "Wuusssshhhuu! Wuusssshhhuu!" The explosive snorts were repeated as the deer escaped.

"Whoa!" shouted the alarmed Rob-me. "What the ...?" Turning to the Fearless Leader, the amazed and somewhat frightened Rob-me blurted out, "What the HELL was that?"

The Fearless Leader responded without a second's hesitation, "You're the new deer biologist. You tell me!"

"Sounded to me like she had something stuck in her throat or she blew her nose as hard as she could," said the traumatized agent. "At least there was a lot of air coming out of someplace!"

Our Fearless Leader has been

known to yield to temptation and responded innocently, "That's exactly right! I'm surprised you haven't read about it already. It's a defense mechanism they use when they can't hide or sneak away like they normally do. They just blow their nose in the direction of a suspected source of immediate danger."

"WHAT!" responded the still shaken Rob-me. "You mean …"

"That's right, my man," related the amused Fearless Leader. "She was launching goobers at us!"

"Bullshit!" chortled the insurance man without hesitation.

"I can't believe you have never heard about deer shooting snot rockets," replied the Fearless Leader calmly.

"Oh man, you're putting me on again, you son-of-a-gun," he responded. "You're kidding me, right … snot rockets? I may have been born at night, but it wasn't **last** night."

"For real, man. You see it confuses the deer's predators, especially if they take a direct hit. The loud, scary sound accompanied by the flying goobers gives the deer time to get away before the predator figures out what the heck happened."

"Are you trying to tell me that's a natural deer defense mechanism? That's a bunch of BS!"

"It worked on you, didn't it?" responded the Fearless Leader, his dimples deepening.

Rob-me stared at him. "Well, I guess so but …"

"You know I wouldn't lead you astray, would I?" said the Fearless Leader.

"Now I really don't believe you," replied Rob-me. "Animals don't do that kind of stuff. Snot rockets? That's a bunch of baloney."

"Oh yeah?" remarked the confident Fearless Leader. "Haven't you been telling me all about deer behavior? Like when they stare at each other and lay their ears back on their heads as a sign of aggression, and how about when they stand on their hind legs and flail their hooves at each other on occasions?"

"Yeah, that's true enough, but snot rockets?"

"Sure, lots of animals have those kinds of defense mechanisms," replied the Dean of the Outdoors. "Bears growl and lunge, gorillas cup their hands and slap their chest, chimps slap the ground and shake trees, 'possums play dead, and rattlesnakes rattle. Now try to tell me they don't."

"Okay, but they don't do anything that involves flinging body fluids at you like shooting a snot rocket," insisted the flabbergasted Rob-me. "Do you think I just fell off of the turnip truck or what?"

"Well, how about skunks spraying you with perfume? And how about an octopus squirting ink to confuse its predators, and llamas spit, and horned toads squirt blood from their eyes, and spitting vipers shoot their venom into people's faces? How about those body fluids, professor?"

"Okay, you may be right about those animals, but I can't see a deer shooting a goober at you. No way am I gonna believe that one." He was laughing now. "You guys enjoy teasing me, but I ain't buying that crap!" His infectious laughter was escalating. "I never heard anything like that noise before. I haven't been scared like that in a long time. A couple more incidents like that and I am gonna give up on this deer hunting stuff. Let's get the heck out of here before something else weird happens."

They returned to the truck, tossed their jackets in the bed and headed for the Fearless Leader's house. Returning the way they had departed, they were like two kids who enjoyed playing in the woods. Of course, their rowdy laughter gave away their arrival to the Fearless Leader's wife as they pulled into the driveway a short while later.

"Have a seat you bozos and I'll get you juveniles some milk and cookies," she said as they entered the door. She was a good sport and, thanks to many years of experience, she could spar with the best of the hooligans from the Fearless Leader's gang.

"I gotta go take a whiz," said Rob-me as he departed for the bathroom while tossing his jacket on the kitchen counter as the Fearless Leader and his bride chatted. They had known each other since high school and were both free-spirited and fun-loving people.

When Rob-me returned, Mrs. Fearless Leader remarked, "Hey Robbie, I just tossed your new camo jacket in the washer. I don't know where you children have been, but it had some yucky stuff all over the front of it."

"What the …?" Rob-me came to an abrupt halt as he entered the kitchen and stared at her in disbelief. "You're really kidding me – right?"

"You heard me, silly. Your new jacket is a mess," she responded.

"What kind of stuff?" he asked with obvious skepticism. "What did it look like?"

"Like a big gob of gooey stuff," she replied. "Issh!"

Rob-me's eyes were wide with disbelief.

The Fearless Leader's dimples were deepening, and his eyes were shining as he casually reached for another warm molasses cookie and simply proclaimed with obvious delight, "Bulls eye!"

Holding the Winning Ticket

Social highlights in the great North Country include annual banquets sponsored by the many fine sporting organizations dedicated to wildlife conservation. Not only do the banquets raise lots of money for wildlife, but they also provide a great deal of fun, entertainment and fellowship. And for one special attendee it turned out to be a night to remember.

Rows of eight-foot tables loaded with quality outdoor merchandise of all types stood for everyone to admire. Shopping for weeks, our Fearless Leader, Digger, Moose Rider and their spouses had purchased the fantastic prizes that would be sold, given away or auctioned throughout the evening and into the snowy night.

Hawking raffle tickets were a dozen attractive young ladies who came dressed to the nines, which is a higher degree than when they are out on the town with their significant others. Silent auctions were being readied, and adult refreshments were flowing. Volunteers hurriedly checked pages of inventory, and merchandise was properly marked to make sure that all was in order. Making mental notes to himself, the auctioneer examined each item soon to be put on the block. The annual North

Country extravaganza was getting underway.

Having been served roast beef and all the trimmings, occupants of the smoke-filled room were buzzing with anticipation. Friendly and energetic conversation flowed as new acquaintances were made and old ones renewed. Spouses commented on the sparkling jewelry and shiny glassware. They expressed their preferences and voiced their desires of winning one of the treasures as a door prize.

Rounds of drinks were purchased and consumed by the mixed tables of loggers, businessmen, retirees, union members and spouses. There are no stripes on the sleeves of those who participate in these fun-filled banquets. These are nights to remember, events that bring disparate groups together in a community; similar to the way deer hunting unites people who otherwise have nothing much in common. As a new member of the community and the deer-hunting group headed by our Fearless Leader, I felt rich.

Whoops and hollers, in addition to rounds of applause intermixed with a few catcalls, continued throughout the evening as the outdoor treasures were dispersed. The Fearless Leader's wife won a case of motor oil, and he won a glass figure of a doe and her fawn.

"We'll negotiate a trade when we get home," beamed the Fearless Leader.

"Good luck!" was her reply. "I'll have a headache by then. And, come to think of it, so will you, but you'll still have yours in the morning." The rest of the members seated at the table roared.

Meanwhile Bebe's wife won two boxes of 20-gauge steel shot, and Swamp Swede was the new owner of a woman's turtleneck sweater. Neither knew what they would do with their prizes, but both were pleased and were having a great time.

"Whoop-tee-do!" exclaimed the jocular Bink, who quickly sold the new camo cigarette lighter he had won to Marty for 10 bucks. "Whoop-tee-do!" Twiggy wasn't about to sell his prize; a gift certificate from the sport shop for a new Speedo.

Elated with winning a framed print of a massive 12-point buck with symmetrical drop tines, Moose Rider exclaimed, "This is great! I've got a spot for it right next to the fireplace." It would look good in his homemade log cabin.

Toward midnight, the coveted limited edition shotgun was about to be given away. One last parade of the appealing, but tired-looking young ladies and the hall became quiet as the tickets were drawn from deep within the wire cylinder.

"Three ... six and ... four," shouted the emcee as he read the numbers of the lucky ticket. Pausing briefly to add to the anticipation, he slowly revealed the last three numbers, "and a seven ... a niner ... and the final number is a two."

"Yes! Yes! Yes!" came a response from the right corner of the hall. "That's my number!" shouted one of our regional game wardens. Polite applause was intermixed with a few friendly comments and jibes. One local demanded another number to be drawn. Someone felt the rascal had been getting cocky as his retirement approached.

As is true with all wardens, he had faced some challenging and uncomfortable situations during his career. Once, for example, he checked the stringer of the Fearless Leader and his son, "Bear." It seems that the largemouth bass that Bear had joyously caught was a half-inch short of being legal. Writing the ticket was difficult since he knew that everyone in town would hear about the citation, and some would be upset. Some were.

Donating hundreds of hours working on programs like "Hunters for the Handicapped" had won the warden respect, but that was erased instantly in the minds of a couple folks over Bear's incident. Having conducted numerous gun safety classes and having secured game enforcement dollars for the region, the warden also participated in a regional sting operation that sent five serious game offenders to jail. Looking forward to retiring and traveling to warmer climates, he felt wounded by the harsh criticism he received over Bear's ticket.

Now the Fearless Leader and his troops understood the situation and held no animosity toward the warden. Nonetheless, it seemed to further stimulate their creativity in plotting pranks to play on him if the opportunity arose. The warden was well aware of that fact.

Offered high-fives as he made his way to the front of the hall to claim his valuable prize, he held the brand-new gun high over his head. "Yes!" he repeated. "Watch out, you guys!" he exclaimed as he passed the Fearless Leader's table. "Now I can really shoot you clowns in the shorts!"

At his table, the warden joined his buddies who pounded him on the back and playfully tried to wrestle the gun away from him. He had gone to the banquet alone since his wife was out of town, and so he found himself at a table full of guys, usually the most unruly place to be at the banquet. The Fearless Leader sent one of the ticket sellers for a beer for the warden, and shortly thereafter, Moose Rider purchased a round for the warden's entire table. "I've never seen you tightwads so generous," commented the surprised and jubilant tee-totaling warden. "I may even miss you rascals after I retire ... or maybe not!" He grinned.

As the final mallard prints and matched cutlery were auctioned off, and the silent auction came to an end, I heard shouting and giggling emanating from the Community Center telephone booth. It was the familiar voice of our Fearless Leader. Seeing me, he opened the door, and I could see that his dimples were showing. "Hey, Doc, go tell Moose Rider to find me a Phillips screwdriver. Quick!" One never knew what he was up to. One learned not to ask.

Another round of beer was sent to the warden's table, and he was having a hard time trying to escape to go home. As you may suspect, friends told him not to even think of leaving as long as he was attracting rounds of beer. Furthermore, he was waiting for the Fearless Leader to find the box which belonged to the new shotgun. But the Fearless Leader was running in three different directions with a full can of beer, and his laughter reverberated as he went from group to group to converse. Stopping at the warden's table, he explained that he couldn't find the box in all of the confusion but promised to locate it and drop it off at the warden's home the next morning.

An hour later, into the darkness and cold went the exhausted warden toting his new shotgun and other winnings: a mallard in flight engraved in the bottom of an ashtray, a gallon of bar oil for a chainsaw, and an insulated travel mug from Rob-me's insurance agency. His car engine cranked slower than normal in the cold night. Sputtering at first, his engine caught and began to idle normally while emitting a visible vapor plume from the exhaust pipe into the frigid night air. Allowing the vehicle to warm for three or four minutes, he then eased the stiff car out onto the highway. But before he reached the next intersection, red and blue flashing lights illuminated the snow-covered landscape.

By some strange "coincidence," the local constable was in the area and noticed the warden's car leaving the Community Center without a taillight on the passenger side. Nobody knows exactly how the conversation went for sure, but we were able to reconstruct something like the following:

"Something wrong, constable?"

"Oh! Hi warden. I noticed that you are missing a taillight, so I pulled you over."

"You're kidding! I didn't know I had a light out."

"You been at the big doings tonight at the hall?"

"Yep! Had a great time. Pretty lucky, too!"

"That so? Tell me, did you have anything to drink?"

"Well, yes ... I had a beer and some sips from a couple others but ..."

"So, you have been drinking and now you're driving. Have

you had enough to impair your driving ability?"

"Oh, hell no! You know me better than that."

"You don't have an open container in the car do you?" inquired the constable with a concerned look on his face.

"You've got to be kidding! Take a look if you want."

As he aimed the six-celled flashlight into the back seat, the yellowish beam immediately came to rest on the new shotgun.

"Say, what's this?" asked the constable with curiosity. "An uncased firearm?"

"Oh man! I just won it, and they couldn't find the box it came in, so I just put it in the back seat and … well, I was going straight home. The bride is out of town and … Oh man! Come on constable."

"Well, here's the way I see it. You've got a taillight out, you've been drinking and driving, and you have an uncased firearm in the backseat of your car. I think you had better go back to the Community Center and see if somebody will give you a ride home."

"What the …? Come on! Give me a break," pleaded the weary warden.

"I could think about writing you a citation. Multiple citations, as a matter of fact!"

"Oh, come on! I can't believe this is happening," moaned the warden.

Back they went, and it was amusing to see how the tired warden's eyes quickly scanned the room. Seeing the Fearless Leader's wife, he immediately and discreetly asked if she would take him home. Being a caring person, she occasionally was asked to chauffeur anyone who was in need of such services. The warden would certainly not ask anyone from the Fearless Leader's party lest he bear the brunt of considerable and long-termed flak.

As the dejected and embarrassed warden and Mrs. Fearless Leader departed out the front door of the hall, the constable turned and winked at the Fearless Leader, Digger and Moose

Rider. The Fearless Leader's dimples were showing, and Digger was cackling his falsetto laugh while Moose Rider was tossing and catching a small object in his big hand. I couldn't say for sure, but it looked something like a glass bulb one might find in a car's taillight.

Spooky Buck Incident

His voice sounded like a rusty file rubbing against polished steel, and distress exuded from every disjointed sentence as he struggled to explain what had happened. By the way, it really did happen.

"It's been right here in the living room where everyone could see it, and I shot the son-of-a-gun."

"What was it?" asked our Fearless Leader with growing concern.

Ignoring the question, he continued to ramble. "I don't know if it's a message from the deer gods or not, but I haven't slept well for three friggin' nights, not since I shot it." Speaking at the other end of the phone line was an uneasy, unsure and unnerved Moose Rider. These were characteristics one never would use to describe this extraordinary man. He was the consummate deer hunter, the leader of family outings, and the one who had grown up in the North Country along with the Fearless Leader ... instigator of most everything.

"I've got to talk to some of my Indian friends to see how they interpret it and see what they think I should do. Maybe the deer gods are trying to tell me that this is my last buck, or maybe it's an omen of something worse."

"Maybe you're overreacting a little," cautioned the Fearless Leader. "Maybe you …"

Cutting him off, Moose Rider rambled on aimlessly. "I know it means something, and I've tried to think of all the signs they've explained to me in the past. I've been racking my brain, but I can't think of anything that's like this."

"Maybe you're overreacting a little," the Fearless Leader repeated in a futile attempt to get Moose Rider to listen.

Sighing deeply, Moose Rider said, "I gotta find out what this all means." He hung up without saying anything more.

The incident began innocently enough at the annual white-tail hunter's banquet held at the town's community center. Saving his money for months in hopes of outbidding our Fearless Leader for the coveted Terry Redlin print, Moose Rider dropped out after the bidding reached a thousand bucks. Disappointed, he purchased a hundred dollars worth of "Chinese auction" tickets and thrust the tickets into waiting containers like a songbird feeding its hungry chicks. When the winning tickets were drawn, Moose Rider had won a framed print of an impressive 12-point buck. Appearing handsome, stately, authoritative and confident, the deer in the picture portrayed all the characteristics he admired in a dominant buck. Some say that we admire the same qualities in an animal that we want others to see in us. But no one, not even stately bucks are perfect, as the artist had suggested. He gave the massive buck two long drop-tines, one on each side.

Hanging on the wall, the new print was the perfect addition to the mounted rainbow trout, carved mallard decoys, and framed duck stamps used to decorate Moose Rider's log cabin. Cutting the huge pine trees himself, he had constructed the stately home on land purchased from "Digger," the local real estate agent. Occupying a space to the right of the fieldstone fireplace, which he also constructed from local materials, the new print filled the spot reserved for the 6 x 6 elk mount. However, elk hunting was a couple years in the future, and deer season opened the Saturday before his disjointed phone call.

The traditional case-of-beer wager for the biggest buck of the season was on with the Fearless Leader, and the friendly sparring had already begun. All was well in the North Country. Ten whole days to deer hunt. He thrived on the usual pressure of judging whether to ignore the lesser bucks in hopes of beating the Fearless Leader out of the brewskies.

Wandering under Moose Rider's stand on Monday was a lucky basket-shaped six-pointer. It would be allowed to walk and live for another day. Catching a glimpse of a stately buck late Tuesday, he saw little more than a shadow in the twilight. Could it have been a 10 or 12 pointer that would have been sufficient to bring home the case of brews? Sleep eluded Moose Rider that night as he mulled over various hunting strategies in his mind. "I now know how my students used to feel when they were cramming their brains for my final exam," said the part-time junior college instructor.

Wednesday's partly cloudy forecast turned into six inches of partly cloudy on the ground by morning, making a snow-depth total of nearly a foot at the National Weather Service site a few miles away. Crunching through the fresh snow and reaching his tree stand well before dawn, Moose Rider said he had that sixth sense that something was going to happen that morning.

Shortly before 10 o'clock in the grayness of the chilly morning, slight movement caught his eye, and he strained to decipher some hint of deer anatomy in the snow-covered branches and undergrowth. Picking out a couple of bold upright tines, he saw that they were large in diameter and could possibly belong to a Boone and Crockett buck. But only a small part of the buck's body could be seen. Not enough to risk a shot.

Catching another glimpse, he saw the creature silently pushing his way through the tangle like a ghostly demon in the night.

Stalking as only a smart old buck can do, he advanced without sound or disturbing the snow-laden branches. He picked his route with such alertness and cunning that Moose Rider knew he was observing a trophy without actually seeing the secretive animal. Raising his rifle in anticipation, he watched in slow-motion, heart-pounding agony.

A brief show of a rut-swollen neck, and Moose Rider did not hesitate. Snow cascaded down limbs as the big brute thrashed though the underbrush and disappeared into heavy cover.

After he regained his composure, Moose Rider climbed down and easily followed the trail in the snow. He approached the massive buck with the complex, conflicting feelings that invariably accompany harvesting such a tremendous animal.

Lying on its right side with the front of its head half-buried in snow, the slain Goliath did not move. The buck had pushed forward until the very end. Stooping over and wrapping his shaking hand around the stocky antler base, Moose Rider saw that it possessed a long drop-tine. His hand barely reached all the way around the antler. With admiration he lifted the fallen buck's head. That's when he froze. The left antler was identical to the right, drop-tine and all. He had dispatched a buck with atypical antlers identical to the framed print he had just won at the banquet! That had been the incident that rattled Moose Rider.

Seeking spiritual advice, Moose Rider consulted his long-time Native American friend, "Sam Two-Dogs", with whom he had hunted deer and fished for brook trout throughout northwestern Wisconsin. Sam was given his traditional name after two dogs were observed by his father as the baby boy came screaming into the world. That's part of the story, anyway.

Having a strong bond to his family traditions and his people's lore, Sam was the logical person for Moose Rider to consult regarding his quandary. Listening as intently as he would for the fragile sound of a wood thrush, Sam's doe-like eyes seemed to empathize with the Moose Rider's dilemma. After careful deliberation and spending a day alone in his canoe on the St. Croix flowage in Douglas County while dressed in his grandfather's beaded leather shirt, he spoke these words softly and emotionally to Moose Rider: "There are many things about such events that we do not understand and cannot comprehend, but such is the beauty of Nature. Do not be frightened by what you do not understand. How can man possibly understand the ways of Nature when he cannot understand his own feelings about the hunt? Do not despair, honor the deer and honor the spirits of the land."

While awaiting the return of the mount from the local taxidermist, Moose Rider had plenty of time to contemplate the strange situation that had befallen him and to reflect on Sam Two-Dog's advice.

Being an accomplished wildlife artist, he visualized a plan from many different angles and attitudes. On a sub-zero day in February when the drop-tine buck was delivered to his log home, Moose Rider hung the awesome mount next to the print with identical antlers in the spot reserved for the 6 x 6 elk.

Smiling as he sat before the cabin's massive fireplace, he opened the last cold bottle of a certain adult beverage. Holding the brown bottle up above his head, he saluted the buck mount in his own traditional way and simply said, "Thanks." He had recovered from his peculiar ordeal, and he had saved the bottle especially for this occasion. It was a special bottle. It was the last one of the prized 24 – compliments of our Fearless Leader.

Two of a Kind

Deer hunting in the North Country on a day with light drizzle falling can be rewarding, although sometimes depressing. It can lower one's spirits and expectations, not to mention tolerance for sitting in a damp tree stand when one could be sitting in front of a warm, inviting fireplace. Both being avid whitetail bowhunters, they knew that they had to pay their dues once in a while, so they met early in the misty morning in spite of the negative weather forecast. They quietly trudged up the 200-foot aspen- and birch- covered hill to their pre-selected hunting sites. They were brothers in the hunt.

One could not actually see the light drizzle falling, but it could be felt. Leaves recorded its presence, and the rain's collective energy made a slight hissing sound when it wasn't masked by the variable winds blowing over Lake Superior about 50 miles to the northwest. Moisture intensified the tangerine and crimson colors of the autumn leaves amidst straggling green leaves that seemed to flaunt their rapidly deteriorating chlorophyll. Dark, earthy colors of the bark and stems were also heightened, and the rain nourished the flourishing lichens that clung to them for life. Large droplets intermittently fell from a leaf or naked stem and splattered with audible force.

Leaves had already fallen from the hawthorns, always the first to shed their foliar responsibility. Maples were releasing their colorful remnants one at a time, as if trying to delay the approaching winter. Acorns cut loose by energetic squirrels could also be heard as they fell from the mighty oaks.

Reaching his deer stand first, Moose Rider gingerly climbed up and settled in. Pulling his collar snug around his neck provided protection from the cool breeze and scattered droplets of precipitation. On his head he wore a mountain man's hat lined with coyote fur. He made the hats during the long North Country winter for entertainment and profit by combining his trapping skills with his artistic creativity. They are in high demand locally.

Knowing that deer would be working their way uphill to take advantage of uplifting air currents and, given the wet ground cover, he would have to remain acutely alert. He opened his stainless steel thermos and poured hot ginger tea into his cup. The brew warmed his fingers and his outlook. He watched his companion continue up the hill and then lost sight of him in the mist and multicolored forest. A blue jay called.

Bebe is the younger of the two hunters, as Moose Rider often reminds him. Carrying his jacket beneath his arm, he absorbed the dampness of the morning but knew he would overheat if he climbed the hill wearing the protective clothing.

Hunting was something they had done together since they were youngsters. Knowing the terrain and the whitetail's habits, he was relaxed as he climbed into position and arranged his bow-hunting gear to his satisfaction. He looked toward his older brother's stand. Although he could not see it through the mist, he knew its exact location. Opening and thumbing through his tattered volume of Robert Service's poetry, he quickly realized that the precipitation was too heavy and returned the worn book to his small, weather-beaten Duluth Pack. He'd revisit it and commit more verses to memory if the drizzle stopped while he hunted.

There was no competition between the brothers over bragging rights for the biggest buck. Well, that is not entirely correct. It is perhaps more accurate to say that there were no longstanding wagers as there were between Moose Rider and our Fearless Leader. This was family hunting and each would be proud of the other's success. Similarly, each would benefit at family gatherings or events that required them to bring venison summer sausage or a huge steaming pot of tasty venison chili. This hunt was about brothers acquiring food supplies for the winter, the same activity in which the squirrels were engaged, despite the drizzle.

Not attempting to read as his brother did, Moose Rider was content to study his surroundings. Without doubt, given the sky conditions and forecast, bluebills would be on the move. Racing in at top speed and making a sound like the tearing of canvas, they would brush the treetops and drop onto the surface of one of the many pothole lakes that dot the northwestern Wisconsin landscape. Moose Rider said that duck recipes were scrolling through his mind when the unmistakable nasal call of a red-breasted nuthatch got his attention and reminded him he was hunting whitetail bucks. He concentrated on his surroundings.

Listening to the rich mixture of autumn sounds was a favorite fall pastime of Moose Rider. He could distinguish between the rustling of dry fallen leaves by a squirrel as it buried its harvest, and the sound of a mouse or shrew darting to safety. He knew the audible pattern of cautious ruffed grouse trekking on dry leaves. But the dampness of the morning worked against his knowledge and experience and gave the animals an added advantage. He had told his younger brother that he would have to focus on seeing motion instead of relying on noises because of the adverse conditions.

However, it was the sound of a deer thrashing through the woods shortly after 10 o'clock that startled his senses. Snorting an alarm in a timid manner, suggesting not only danger but also shock, the deer stumbled downhill as wounded deer are inclined to do. Had Bebe connected? Straining to catch further movements, he heard the unmistakable voice of his brother.

"Tally Ho!"

It was our clan's signal for a successful shot.

"All right!" Moose Rider said out loud as he smiled and prepared to lower his bow and descend from his lofty stand.

"Which way did he go?" asked the Moose Rider as he reached the ground and leaned his bow against a sturdy maple. "Big one, Bebe?"

"I think he went right down that gully and dropped pretty quickly. He's a good one," responded Bebe as he came down the hill and pointed to the small ravine to the east of his brother's tree stand. Exchanging high-fives, they walked together in the direction of the ravine, each wearing a broad smile.

"I think he was an eight-pointer. He was making his way through that thick stuff but never made a sound. I wouldn't have seen him if he hadn't given himself away by grunting at a little doe he was following. He didn't rustle a leaf or anything," said Bebe. "But he made the mistake of grunting."

"With that wet forest floor, you aren't gonna hear them walking for sure. Good job, Bro!"

They found the fallen eight-point buck in the shallow ravine and tagged it right away. Each one holding a symmetrical polished antler, they easily dragged him out into the open.

"Let's get him taken care of," said Moose Rider, "he ain't a Pope and Young buck, but he's a doggoned good one. He'll be a good eater."

"You wanna quit now and register him or stay for a while?" asked Bebe as he removed his hunting knife from its protective camo case and tested its edge for sharpness.

"It's still early. After we're done guttin' him, why don't you go back and get the truck and throw on a pot of chili at the house?

We'll stop by the check station on the way to lunch. Let's pull him on over by my stand and I'll stay here and hunt until you get back in an hour or so."

Upon completing the gutting task, they dragged the buck downhill. Propping up the buck's head, Bebe smiled for a quick snapshot from the disposable camera his brother carried for such occasions. He then set off to retrieve his gear and waved as he ambled downhill to the vehicle.

Meanwhile, Moose Rider settled back into his deer stand. He sighed as he looked around as individual leaves fell gently to the ground. He would wait for Bebe and help him with the buck. They would feast on spicy venison chili for lunch; the only kind of chili there is, as far as the brothers were concerned. He wished he had told his younger brother to bring back a bottle of schnapps for a toast to a successful hunt.

Light drizzle continued, and the woods whispered shyly. Then the droplets turned into imperfect snow pellets that bounced and ricocheted on impact. Bluebills tore through the low, scudding clouds as the experienced hunter had predicted. The sky had not brightened but his spirits had.

He thought of the chili and his brother's luck. Looking down at the buck's carcass, he smiled, and his thoughts turned to other hunts they had shared. As the oldest he had taught his brother everything he knew about the ways of the whitetail. He enjoyed sharing his knowledge and had once considered moving down-state to teach at the university. In the end, he chose to remain in the North Country. His wandering mind was on a previous hunt where someone had burned a pot of chili beyond recognition, when an intense buck grunt shattered his peaceful daydreaming. It was so close!

A red squirrel scolded furiously. Freezing at the sound of the danger signals, the hunter's heart raced as his brain struggled to unscramble the alarm messages. Turning his head ever so slowly he spied an annoyed 11-point buck eyeing Bebe's fallen animal with obvious agitation.

Stamping his feet, the buck grunted a second time and jerked his massive head up high to inhale the damp air. The hair on his back stood erect, and his wet nostrils flared as he twitched his tail. Walking two steps toward the prone deer, the huge buck stamped his foot sharply. A mere 25 feet separated the two deer, and the distance decreased with each nervous step. Rapidly repositioning his head up and down, the angry buck advanced as he apparently tried to analyze the puzzling situation.

Lowering his dark antlers as if to charge the reclining eight-pointer, the bigger buck pawed the ground and took a couple more steps, but he never took his eyes off of his rigid foe. The enraged buck's ears were flattened against his body. He was indeed ready to attack! Again he grunted.

Recognizing that flattened ears are a sure indicator of intense aggression, Moose Rider knew the challenger would not spook easily. He had ample time to make one good shot count. The irate buck was going nowhere.

Regaining his senses, Moose Rider fought to breathe normally and managed to draw the lethal arrow back without incident. The unlucky buck might not have been observed if he had not challenged the lesser buck lying prone on the ground. The bigger buck was overcome with the urge to become king-of-the-hill, the biological struggle of survival-of-the-fittest. Moose Rider certainly did not hear the angry buck approaching until it grunted. It was the kind of situation for which hunting magazines could not have prepared a hunter, but now there were two nice bucks on the ground. Two bucks had made fatal audible mistakes on a damp, drizzly North Country morning. They were two of a kind.

Deer Hunting Rituals

"So, how serious is it?" she was asking the Moose Rider's better-half as I was rummaging through the cluttered kitchen drawer. "Do you think he'll survive another year?" And after a pause, she continued, "Oh! You bet'cha. He's got the same symptoms, too. I'll be glad when it's finally over with. Maybe we can get some peace and quiet then. In the meantime, just try to be patient and hope they don't do anything too stupid." I quickly retreated to the safety of the basement.

The earliest symptoms begin to appear as autumn approaches and the daylight hours become shorter, according to the bride. She says that my telephone calls become more frequent and last longer than usual. The lengthy conversations – so she says – are conducted in low voices but there are also periods of childish giggling toward the end. She insists that sporting catalogues, hunting magazines, and wildlife videos start to pile up around the house, and the checkbook is likely to get out of whack at that time of year. Funny, I never noticed!

"Your mind is preoccupied, and you act irresponsibly. I mean, more than usual," adds the lady of the house. "And then it gets worse!"

"When a lot of strange grunting sounds and rattling noises start coming from the basement, and the closets and dresser drawers look like the Bureau of ATF has searched through them, it's a sure sign that deer season is approaching," claims the missus.

I can't deny that fact; a deer hunter's addiction gets worse every year. My topo maps are spread out on the floor every night for weeks. My late night guests and I search for saddles and funnels and other promising land features. Practicing the art of antler rattling at that time of night has gotten me into trouble more than once. Moose Rider is usually the perpetrator!

Meanwhile, countless hours are spent searching high and low for missing gear. So what if a petrified cookie or two and the remains of a year-old candy bar or stick of jerky land on the kitchen counter when I clean out my pack? What's the big deal?

The final stages of deer hunting preparation – according to the spouse – although I hotly contest her observation, includes a period of being extra nice that may include washing the dishes or taking out the trash without having been asked three times. She contends that it's a part of a predictable behavior pattern observed when one desires to make a major purchase, like a new deer rifle or a climbing tree stand.

I will admit that I make a lot of extra trips to the Fearless Leader's sport shop during the weeks when the temperature plummets and the leaves turn yellow. But as far as sucking up to diffuse the impact of a major purchase, deer hunters would never dream of such a thing. Would we?

"A spouse who has a birthday or anniversary just before hunting season starts has it made," asserts the woman. But only if they know how to play their cards." Oh! How I hate to be manipulated.

Planning the hunting trip is a major element of the tradition. I think it's a part of the primordial urge passed on in our genes. Picture early man sitting by the campfire chipping away at a flint to form a primitive arrowhead or spear. No doubt his hunting buddies join him, and they draw maps and plot their strategy in the dirt with smoldering sticks from the fire. Surely they brag about previous hunts and draw pictures of deer on the sides of cliffs and on the walls of their caves. I wonder if any pictographs have been discovered that show a man riding on the back of a moose? I also wonder if their significant others nagged at them about their deer hunting rituals?

While the articles on the list of gear have changed, the art of preparing for the hunt remains a talent to be admired. Instead of packing stone arrowheads with willow arrow shafts, animal skin clothes and knowledge of the terrain, we now pack carbon arrows with titanium tips, scentless computer-generated camouflage clothes with high-tech insulation and an expensive GPS. My list of gear for deer camp is even computerized. Can you imagine what a stag-hunting Neanderthal would think about that?

Regardless of the time spent preparing for the hunt, at least one item is sure to be overlooked. Something escapes the diligent effort of the most meticulous planner. A friend once forgot the gas tanks for his outboard on our way to a northern moose hunt, and we had to beg one from a nearby resort. But those events help make for a memorable hunt.

Don't forget about all of the new hunting gadgets like a tilt-compensated electronic compass or a voice-activated programmable 14- channel two-way radio. No list is ever complete. For it is part of the tradition. One has to buy new gadgets to be fully prepared for deer hunting.

During those last days and hours before the long-awaited departure for deer camp – on both sides of the matrimonial aisle, I might add – comes the series of "my" questions:

Have you seen my ...?

Will you help me find my ...?

Will you wash my ...?

What did you do with my ...?

Will you sew up my ...?

Why can't I find my ...?

Around our house, there may be a frantic, "What the hell did you do to my ...?" I remember the time my polypropylene long-johns were dried in the clothes dryer and shrank to a size to fit an eight-year-old. Another trip to the Fearless Leader's sports shop!

But for all the effort put into the preparations, the spouse unjustifiably claims that I don't have nearly as much enthusiasm for putting the same deer hunting stuff away when I come home from deer camp. Imagine that!

I overheard the bride say to Moose Rider's wife shortly after the hunt ended, "I don't know what's worse" – as I was hastily dumping another load of clothes embedded with a wonderful aroma of cigar smoke, stale beer and perhaps a little doe-in-estrous scent – "the mess they make before leaving or the mess they bring home."

"Maybe we should try to get them to take up bowling next year, instead," she continued. "But, on second thought, it's sure nice to get them out of the house for a whole week when the symptoms strike and they turn into little boys again. Let's have coffee soon and, by the way, when **does** next year's deer season start? I can hardly wait!"

Reflections of Night Eyes

Sitting on the edge of the ancient Plymouth's worn cloth seat in anticipation, the bashful six-year-old peered wide-eyed into the autumn darkness. Searching the outer edges of the glowing beams of light from the old car's headlights as it topped a hill or rounded a curve, he was developing an early love for viewing wildlife. He was intent on spotting a pair of green or yellow reflections that would stimulate that unlimited imagination of youth and fill him with mixed emotions of wonder, excitement, awe and fear.

There was always a contest to see which one of us siblings would claim the coveted front seat between our parents. I suppose it was primarily for attention, but it was also warmer near the vintage car's heater, the old man used with great reluctance.

"Cuts down on the gas mileage too much," he claimed. As you may have already guessed, we were living in the middle of the conservative Midwestern Bible Belt. Dad had grown up during the Great Depression.

For me, the primary reason to claim the front seat was hunting. I wanted to catch a glimpse of those intriguing eyes that belonged to the wild creatures that come out at night when men are afraid. I couldn't get enough.

Visiting my aunt and uncle's modest farm in central Indiana was my favorite hunting trip. On those memorable trips to their homestead, I fished for bullheads with my cousin under the tiny bridge on the lonely county road, collected the tadpoles of leopard frogs along the meandering creek, and shot a cowbird with my new BB gun. Once I found an arrowhead while searching for them with my dad in a newly plowed cornfield. I was fascinated to learn that Native Americans hunted with them.

Relaxing on lazy summer days in the hayloft of the old red barn, I dreamed of hunting with the relatives when they made rare trips to the North Country. But the highlight of the visit was always the trip home. Much of the route was over dusty, gravel-covered county roads. At that time, brushy fence rows still existed between the plowed fields and backroads and, to my young impressionable mind, the wildlife that lived along the edges was as mystical and wild as wolves.

So what if the wild animals were raccoons, skunks and 'possums instead of wolves, bears and deer? To me they represented wildness. And the bigger and brighter the night eyes, the better. I cherished the hunt.

To spy a bounding whitetail was rare in those days. That is a testament to the success of modern wildlife management practices. When I did have the fortune to spot an elusive whitetail, it took my breath away like the shock of a cold shower. Those images of a princely buck bounding gracefully across the roadway or freezing under the hypnotic spell of the headlights still persist. Every hunter I know has similar treasured memories from their childhood.

Now when I drive to pick up the Fearless Leader or "BeBe," my brook trout partner, I always take the backroads when traveling early in the morning or late in the day. Memories of those childhood adventures return each time. I get that old feeling of excitement as soon as the dome light is illuminated and I climb into my pickup's cab. Hunting begins when the beams from the truck's headlights sweep across the dark yard as I leave home. Each trip is a new adventure.

Disappointment arises if the lights from another car appear during my solitary back roads sojourn. It is an unwelcome intrusion. Perhaps I am selfish with my hunting grounds, but I wish I could post a "no trespassing" sign on the road. When the drive is completed and I pick up my passenger, the short return to youth is over. Although we may still see wildlife on our way to our appointment in the woods, it's not the same experience as my solitary hunts.

Seeing any animal at dawn or dusk, even the cunning coyote, is a joy. When that happens during my solo hunts, I actually have a feeling of comradeship. I am happy to have shared that brief moment with the legendary trickster. Although I get a sense of satisfaction knowing that I could have taken him, I am happy just to have spotted him and to know that he spied me. But it's deer that I really want to see.

Observing a handsome buck lowering his head and sneaking off the road or leaping over a barbed wire fence, or when a doe pauses momentarily in the truck's headlights, I stop and roll down the window to watch them if there isn't any traffic. I marvel at their twitching ears, their searching eyes, or a nervous stamping foot. Sometimes I tell them that they had better not make a practice of spending time close to these roads. As they disappear in confused haste, I savor the satisfaction of another successful hunt.

Every wildlife sighting brings me pleasure. But what I value the most is seeing those wondrous, magical eyes illuminated in the headlights of the truck at night – those night eyes that recall and reflect something special from my past.

The Lonesome Road

Driving alone on a long sojourn to deer camp is like hearing the nostalgic whistle of a train in the far distance on a clear, dark and frigid night. There is eagerness to be on the road headed toward an exciting adventure but also melancholy tugging at the heart that yearns for the security and comforts of home.

Packing for deer camp is always a hurried, though essential, chore. Lists are constructed to bring order out of chaos, but there are inevitable last-minute details requiring attention at a time when it is difficult to concentrate. Thoughts are on the whitetails and the companionship that will be experienced while the troops are gathered for our traditional deer hunt. Expectations are lofty. They always are on opening day.

Furthermore, the last night before the departure is always filled with restless anticipation. On the final morning, there is a hasty reloading of the mountain of gear and then a goodbye kiss. Well, by the time one arrives at the first traffic light, there is a mix of emotions, a moment of torture. It's like seeing the warm, inviting glow of cabin lights across the lake as one paddles a canoe toward a wilderness campsite to pitch a solitary tent in the darkness.

How satisfying, though, to leave behind the phone, pager and fax machine. No more e-mails! We will concentrate on deer hunting, and that's it. Sure, communications are available in case of emergency, but the daily newspapers won't find us. And we do not care, thank you very much.

The burdened SUV is jammed full of hunting gear, some of which is actually needed, and my lunch is packed so I will not stop except to refuel or to take a biological break. I listen to the radio and pay attention to world events. Farther down the road, I will stop listening after a final check on the weather forecast. The only thing that will matter tomorrow is the hunt for America's favorite, the white-tailed deer. But that's tomorrow.

As the miles pass, I think of each member of my family and value and appreciate their differences. I think about the times when I could have been a better father. I will miss them and think of them when waiting on the trail to start a deer drive or during a slow, deliberate still hunt early in the morning. The miles parade by like the relived memories. The road is lonesome.

I plan ahead to stop and stretch my weary legs in Madison and take a quick jaunt along the highly tempting isles of a major sporting goods chain store. I also know that I have everything I need, so my only purchase will likely be a bag of candy to pass the time while hunting. The stop will be brief, and I will probably decide on licorice. The red ones.

I set the cruise control to keep from speeding and eagerly look at highway information signs listing the remaining miles to distant cities. Like all hunters, photographers and whitetail watchers, I begin to watch the fence rows and corners of fields for deer. They will be brownish-gray or mousy-gray this time of year, having shed their shorter and thinner reddish-brown hair. How red some of them appear during the summer! How well their winter coats blend into their surroundings during the hunt! Changing, too, at this time of year is their diet. Being opportunistic, they take advantage of what's available and nutritious – mushrooms in the spring, apples and acorns in the fall, and whatever browse they can find during the long North Country winters. They have adapted so well. Perhaps that's part of the reason that the whitetail is our most observed and revered game animal.

The Corn Belt harvest had been good, and the countryside was entering its long period of hibernation. Standing at attention are straight formations of hybrid corn signs marking the successful rows of new varieties. High tech evolution at work.

Miles of urban tracts pass, and I feel sorry for people who are still sleeping and not on the road to deer camp. I feel privileged to be leaving civilization – although that's a questionable term – and heading northward to our primitive shack.

Cars loaded for opening day whiz past in both directions. They stream in single file like herds of migrating caribou seeking fertile grazing grounds. Eighteen-wheelers pass by. I wonder where they are going and what they are hauling. I envy them for being free on the open road. I know they are talking on their CBs about road conditions and seat covers, and I wonder if they are reporting significant buck sightings as well.

Leaving my home state behind, I open a neatly wrapped sandwich. There is the customary bite right out of the middle. She has always done that. A secret message or expression of love, or a plot to make me feel lonesome or guilty about leaving for deer camp for a week?

Crossing the Wabash River at the state line, I notice a sign that advertises the "world's largest fireworks store." I wonder how many identical signs there are. Hundreds, I presume. "The fireworks," I say out loud with a chuckle, "will begin on opening morning."

It is still early enough in the day that I spot three deer grazing in the back of a picked corn field, and I am again reminded of how well whitetails have adapted. Having a four-chambered stomach, they can feed hastily in the open where they are at the highest risk of danger. Returning to the security of heavy cover, they chew their cud like cows and other ruminants. Thus, they can eat fast but still chew their food leisurely to aid in its digestion. We have not fared so well.

The sky is disagreeable and darkening, but I know that the elements will not keep me from reaching deer camp tonight. I will get through. I feel like a sockeye salmon returning to my home stream. I am adamant and driven, there is no turning around.

I pass by a carload of hunters and wave. They stare at me without expression. The car is from Illinois, and I mumble that I should have known.

I decide to stop for coffee and a restroom break after entering Wisconsin. A wise decision. The establishment claims they love to see us smile, but the guy at the counter is about as dynamic and charismatic as a three-toed sloth. He doesn't appear to care whether I smile or not. He hands the coffee to me, turns around and walks away without speaking. I know the buffoon will never be a deer hunter. I smile.

I enter a 16-mile construction zone but do not see a single highway worker, or highway employee for that matter, through the entire zone. Were they all at home packing for deer camp? As the construction-less zone ends, I return to cruising speed and notice that the road conditions have deteriorated significantly. Nonetheless, I feel rejuvenated and consider unleashing the horses under the hood but know that this is the most dangerous part of a hunting trip and resist the urge.

I am eager to get to where birch trees block the field of view instead of highway advertising signs, and where neat stacks of split firewood next to homes outnumber the huge rolls of hay in the fields. Where deer shacks replace farms, and tractors give way to four-wheelers is where I want to be. I look at the clock and find that five minutes have passed since the last time I checked. Three huge raindrops fall on the windshield and slowly drift upward against the pull of gravity. Strong forces are pulling me northward.

Passing a farm with multiple silos and shining conveyors, I see that it is directly across the highway from an abandoned farmstead. An unfriendly and stark contrast, but I think to myself, "what a good place to hunt." Deer love deserted farmsteads, especially those with abandoned apple orchards.

Finally reaching Madison, I miss the poorly marked turn for the sporting goods store and decide the red licorice isn't that important. I opt for a fast-food break directly across the road. I had stopped at this same chain restaurant before and had gotten the wrong order the last two times. Slowly and succinctly I order a cheeseburger with lettuce and mayo. The attendant asks if I mean tomato (for an extra dime). I repeat "mayonnaise, not tomato." I get the lettuce and mayo, but no cheese on my cheeseburger and vow to sell my stock in the company as soon as I return home.

Passing the road that heads north to Rhinelander, I recall my last visit there. Picking up a friend late on a Sunday night at the airport, I found the parking meters all cordoned off with plastic flagging due to construction. So I parked in a rather large lot containing three other cars, only to find that the Northwest flight was late. What's new? Returning to the car after less than five minutes, I found that the city fathers had rewarded my brief visit with a parking ticket. Duh! What don't these cheeseheads understand about tourism? I vowed never to go back and figure I have cost them about $100,000 in lost tourism dollars through my anti-Rhinelander pontifications.

As I grow tired and lonely, my mind wanders. I used to look at license plates to help with the boredom of long distance driving, but now I look at the vehicle's decals of sporting groups or clubs. There is a lot of support from the vehicles heading north, and I am encouraged. On I push, northward.

Passing through Black River Falls – one of my favorite city

names – I see more and more deer-crossing signs and am feeling good about my northward progress. Soon I reach a major milestone when I exit the Interstate at Eau Claire. I see a bumper sticker which reads, "A Woman and Her Truck; It's a Beautiful Thing." The sky clears and the temperature begins to drop as I leave the city limits. I press on.

The number of farms is decreasing, and I soon pass Cranberry Marsh Road and skirt Spooner. After crossing the Namakogon River, I reach the outskirts of our deer hunting territory. My spirits soar as I cross the St. Croix and then brake hard to avoid a doe bounding through the beams of my headlights. I remind her to watch out. The fireworks begin tomorrow. Another great adventure of hunting the white-tailed deer is set to begin, and my anticipation far overshadows the weariness of my tired body.

Stopping at a phone booth before taking the final stretch of backroads to deer camp, I hesitate. The time has come, and I am prepared. That familiar tugging returns when I deposit the coins and shiver in the brisk night air as I dial the phone number. Standing in the clear, dark and frigid night I hear the nostalgic whistle of a train in the far distance.

What's it Worth?

Leaving the confines of the Twin Cities behind, he headed due north on the Interstate toward the Fearless Leader's deer shack. But he made an unanticipated stop that resulted in an increased desire to rush to deer camp. Burning in his mind was an unanswered question. Bolting from the car as it came to a stop; he hurried into the aging cabin. Pleased to see that Bebe was already there, he blurted out the critical question that had obsessed him for the past three hours.

"Do you know what a fox looks like?"

Bebe eyed him with a mix of astonishment and suspicion. "Do I know what a fox looks like? Well, yeah! I know what a fox looks like." A smile came over his face. "Don't you know what a fox looks like?"

"Well, I suppose I do – I just wanted to be totally sure that's what I got."

"Are we talking a four-legged fox or a two-legged fox?" asked Bebe teasingly. He was intrigued.

"Seriously, you sucker; on the way up from home I saw a fresh road kill next to the highway, so I stopped to look it over. I'm pretty sure it's a fox and it's in darned good shape, not much blood or anything, so I put it in the trunk."

"That's against the law, you know," Bebe reminded him while his curiosity increased, and he raised one eyebrow as he does when he is being mischievous.

"Yeah, but it don't make any sense. I mean, it's fall. Pelts are in prime condition, and the fox is just lying there deader than hell. Poor thing must have misjudged the speed of a car and darted out in front of it. Not much of a match between a small animal and a ton of speeding vehicle. Sure seemed like a waste to me to let him stay there and rot."

"You could be the one rotting in jail for just picking it up," continued Bebe.

"Heck I don't know what the animal rights folks would say about that. Do they want to let 'em rot or use the resource for something beneficial like making a hat or something? It's a shame that thousands of animals are hit every year and they just bloat up and waste away – eaten up by maggots."

"Well that's a nice philosophical speech. But you think you've got a dead fox in your trunk?"

The visitor said, "Well, surely it's a fox, but its head isn't real pointed so I thought it might be a coyote."

"The fur is reddish, isn't it? If it's red, it's a fox."

"Yeah, pretty much reddish. I thought it might look good to have it tanned and hang it on the wall or get something made out of it. Maybe even sell it, if it's worth a few bucks."

"They aren't worth as much as they used to be before the antis made an impact on the fur market," said Bebe, who had trapped a great deal when he was growing up in the North Country. "But you can still probably get **something** for it."

"What do you think a fox pelt is worth?"

"Depends on a lot of things – you say it's in good shape?"

"Oh! Heck yeah! It hardly has a mark on it."

"Hair isn't falling out or anything?"

"Oh! Hell no! Come on out and look at it. It's in the trunk of the car right out front."

"Let's go have a look at it then," said Bebe, whose curiosity had piqued.

Bebe wore only shorts and a tee shirt in the cozy, wood-heated shack. He didn't even bother putting on his brown hunting jacket and cap to go outside. Accompanied by Jett, his black Lab and constant companion, he walked to the car that was still pinging rhythmically as the engine cooled from the long trip. Jett sniffed the air with keen interest and then began to inspect the tires.

As the trunk opened, Bebe examined the unfortunate causality and said, "Too bad it didn't live to be full grown. Looks like it would have been a good one all right."

"What's it worth?"

"To tell the truth I doubt if you would get anything for it," responded Bebe.

"Because it's not full grown?"

"Well, that's part of it."

"Did it lie in the road too long?"

"No, the individual hairs don't seem to be loose or anything."

"Well," he spoke while appearing somewhat perplexed. "It is a fox, isn't it?"

"Well, not exactly," said Bebe diplomatically.

"So it is a coyote after all. I suppose they aren't worth as much?"

"Well you see – you just wouldn't get any money for it."

"Why not?" He demanded. "It's a beautiful pelt, and it has a nice color and all. It's in good shape and everything, ain't it?"

"Well, to be honest," said Bebe as he watched his canine companion complete his inspection of the vehicle's tires, "the reason you won't get anything for it is that it's not a fox. And it ain't no coyote either. What you got yourself here, you dummy, is one young and very unlucky golden retriever."

Old Highway A:
The Deer Road

The old highway drew me to it like an emotional magnet. I knew that if I followed her winding path through the North Country I would spot a deer or two. All whitetail watchers have an Old Highway A of their own to visit on special days when they need to fulfill a desire for wildness. I was on a special mission – I knew what I needed – the beautiful and inspiring sight of a white-tailed buck.

Filling up the new TrailBlazer at the service station near the intersection of the old road and the new four-lane highway, I felt like I was at the junction where the road less traveled departs from high-speed travel efficiency. Since I had departed on my sojourn later in the morning than I had intended, my expectations were not high. I had been there before. Still, what a great feeling it was to have begun my journey by leaving the super highway to the speeding tailgate terrorists.

Traveling a scant 30 miles an hour, I spotted a fawn and doe at the far corner of a mowed field within the first mile. Instant success! Like all whitetail observers, I glanced down each dirt road as it crossed Old Highway A in hopes of catching a glimpse of the magnificent *Odocoileus virginanus*. We have all taken a look down those side roads when we were growing up. Often, travel down these paths turns out to be dead ends, but occasional worthwhile ventures help us grow and mature.

Passing a section of mature aspens that had been blown down by the wind, I approached the first "S" curve and crossed the rusty iron bridge. Visions of past hunts came to my mind as I drove across the creek and through a marshy area filled with alders and memories.

I recalled the time when I returned late at night from a South Dakota pheasant hunt, and Highway A was alive with deer. Frequent taps on the brakes were necessary, and each sighting was an awesome new adventure. It seemed a long time ago. Perhaps it was.

Curves in the road are always good places for deer sightings. Rounding each curve offers the opportunity for a new perspective on what is ahead. Hills offer similar opportunities and sur-

prises. Several winters previously, I ascended a hill to find an adult bald eagle feeding on a deer carcass in the middle of the road. It was an unexpected close encounter with nature that I consider one of my favorites.

Glancing down every power line right-of-way is a productive technique for wildlife viewing. They are like visions across time and space, offering both a clear view and the edge effect so important to wildlife. Managing these paths of land through corporate agreements with sportsmen's clubs has resulted in significant wildlife habitat improvements. It makes sense – it all fits together now.

Whoa! A doe ran directly in front of the car, and I hit the brakes hard. It could have been a disaster, but since no one was behind me I sat and waited for more deer to follow her. It's a pattern you come to know. My heart beat fast. I was engrossed with the hunt. The doe ambled off into the bush and vanished like a brook trout released in a North Country stream. She was alone.

Passing Pioneer Trail, I spotted a ruffed grouse next to a well-used deer trail. I have often tried to observe the distant drummer who lives in the black spruce swamp that stretched before me like a welcome mat. I'm still searching. A red-tailed hawk landed high in the tree, hesitated, and then flew away. After watching him go, I soon crossed a creek I had always wanted to fish for brookies – just never took the time. I should have.

Entering the final "S" curve, I passed the Peterson farm where I hunted when I was younger. I spotted a fresh roadkill nearly hidden in the weeds beside the road, an innocent fawn. My final deer sighting was in the rear view mirror as a young buck scampered across the road without looking. Youth! Shortly, I observed a blue heron through the sun roof as I neared the developed lakeshore. It used to be wild but, sadly, no more. I know my trip is coming to an end. I wish it could continue, but I am satisfied.

Around the last curve lies a newly constructed home with

a manicured, fenced yard. The dog kennel and other out buildings are color coordinated. How out of place they looked to me. I have become accustomed to the simple homesteads developed over the years along the old familiar road. I ached for their innocence and lost simplicity.

The Happy Hour Tavern is on my right, and I observe dark rain clouds building to my left. I can't explain why I return to the old road as often as I do. Maybe it isn't a pilgrimage to Mecca or bathing in the Ganges, but each visit leaves me cleansed and revitalized. I had once again seen whitetails as I had in the past. The old road had not let me down. But it also reminds me that things change – including ourselves. As I reluctantly turn off of the old road and approach the four-lane highway, a light drizzle begins to fall.

Paradise Lost

The direction was north, according the Chevy Blazer's electronic compass glowing in the gathering darkness of a November evening. Alongside the iridescent compass, the temperature indicator displayed the current Fahrenheit temperature as "14," the lowest reading thus far during my northward sojourn. I was heading back to the frosty North Country, near the Chequamegon National Forest, to hunt whitetails after being absent for three years. Yet, instead of thinking about deer hunting during the long road trip, my thoughts were on sunny skies, luxurious white sandy beaches, and bronzed bodies.

Undulating coconut palms and gently nodding oleanders mimicked the tropical breeze. Blowing across huge stretches of multicolored Caribbean water, the wind created waves accented by whitecaps, though they were not frightening in intensity. After an hour-long stint on the beach, I had chosen to recline lazily in one of the many connecting waterways of the fresh-water pool surrounded by lush tropical vegetation. It was an exquisite setting. Designer swimwear, fashionable sunglasses and expensive sports cars piloted by tanned bodies came and went. Welcome to paradise.

It had been a Caribbean cruise with a six-day vacation at a luxury resort tacked on the end to allow extra time to celebrate the spring. Celebrate is perhaps a strong word. Lethargy and apathy may be the best words to describe my energy level during those days. At $450 per night, what was one to do to give the false impression of thoroughly enjoying the moment?

Grumpy, gray-haired couples shuffled toward the flashy casino to heedlessly stuff hard-earned money into insatiable one-armed bandits. They gambled to earn the right to grumble, yet it also earned them the right to brag about the great time they had while vacationing in the tropical islands. I didn't get it.

Handsome young men strutting with their chests pushed out beckoned impatiently for apathetic uniformed waiters while seemingly parading trophy companions temptingly dressed in tiny patches of cloth that resembled swimsuits. Touching and posturing, the young crowd bragged of job titles and accomplishments to their friends, as well as to any bystander within hearing range. Like desperate bucks in the grips of the rut – I figured – they were driven by the need to impress others.

A middle-aged couple from Boston, who were delayed for a few minutes while another family boarded the resort's tour bus for a nearby point of non-interest, whined and bellowed because of the wait. Uttering profanity over the delay in front of their children and everyone else on the bus, they must have felt that they were making quite an impression. They were right.

Meanwhile, sun worshipers rubbed lotion on each other and compared their tans like bucks testing antlers in mock battles. Teenaged girls pranced like yearling does while looking over their shoulders to see if any interesting prospects followed their scent trails. Aged men lustily watched the young women through expensive dark sunglasses. However, they stood guard over their own families on the beach like rutting, bull elk protecting their harems.

An attractive young woman with silky blond hair herded

her twin three-year-olds onto an open-air shuttle bus bound for the beach. Shy and obedient, pretty and innocent, they clung to their mother for protection. Her body was tanned and toned, and she wore expensive and fashionable clothes that highlighted her beauty. Her demeanor was pleasant, and her actions refined and graceful as she thumbed through a volume of poetry. She had class. She wore no wedding ring. What had gone wrong? I secretly hoped that she was too normal for this plastic lifestyle.

Yes, that was my visit to paradise. Sun, sand, waves and five-dollar cans of beer. And room service with a three-dollar-per-person delivery charge in addition to a 15 percent gratuity automatically added to your bill "for your convenience." "That's 15 percent minimum," added the lazy, liver-faced attendant as he showed his few remaining discolored teeth. Though harmless I'm sure, he appeared menacing.

It occurred to me that everyone in paradise had at least one thing in common. Nobody appeared to be having a good time, no one smiled. Eye contact was avoided except for a few who possessed cell phones that rang on the beach or played whimsical electronic tones. Their operators glanced about as if to count how many onlookers were impressed by their importance and indispensability. No one occupying the beach chairs shared pleasantries or interests. Actually, there had almost been a fist-fight the previous day over a saved deck chair. The combatants were eye-to-eye and face-to-face like hormone-induced bucks. No signs of dignity or tolerance were obvious. Fight to win. Winner takes all.

Even the resident animals seemed to share the sun worshiper's displeasure. A large black swan with a long, slender neck, far from appearing graceful, seemed threatening and sinister like a cobra ready to strike. It began to chase a smaller swan and stretched its neck out to nip at the tail of the splashing, fleeing youngster. Grackles fought over discarded French fries and shrieked at each other in shrill outbursts while perched on empty beach chairs. How could I forget the commotion?

The Caribbean odyssey, my visit to paradise, had replayed in my mind for the tenth time as I traveled north. Before long, I gratefully tapped the brake pedal to disengage the cruise control and slowed to make the turn off of Highway 53 onto the county road that would lead to the deer shack. I was eager to end my lonesome road trip.

The troops would be waiting. They would be laughing and happily engaged in conversation, sharing family stories and deer hunting tales. They would be enjoying batches of venison sausage and jerky accompanied by Wisconsin cheese. Friends were surely sipping beer, planning deer drives, and having a great time. They would be sharing their love of the North Country and the joys of hunting its wily whitetails. I was thankful that I would soon be joining them for good times. Thoughts of my Caribbean vacation would soon fade. How wealthy I felt to be on the road to deer camp again. Yet, I could not help but feel sorry for the poor, unfortunate folks back in paradise.

No Monkey's Uncle

Blessed are those who hunt deer in traditional family groups! Seems to me that young hunters who have bonded with an uncle at an early age are the most confident, skilled and successful of the traditional family deer hunters. Since that wasn't the case for me, I'm not certain if that assumption has any validity or not. But that's my theory, and I'm sticking to it.

Hunting parties in the North Country have well-defined territories where families have conducted deer drives and built permanent tree stands over the years. Most respectable deer hunters in the region know and honor these family hunting territories as well. Not having to search for a quiet place to hunt must be mighty nice. You know what I'm saying?

Included in many family hunting parties are selected companions with whom relatives have hunted for numerous years and with whom they feel comfortable being together in the woods. Dragging harvested deer out of a dank swamp is a cinch when lots of hunting party members help with the arduous chore; one always accompanied with praise or teasing commentary depending upon the nature of the expired quarry.

Meanwhile, the old men talk of past deer hunts. Listening

with glee, they wink at each other as a young hunter describes rushing a shot and missing a 12 pointer, and isn't it always a 12 pointer that bounds safely into cover? Youngsters have to work their way up the proverbial family hunting tree while witnessing their status elevate with successful hunts or face ridicule with a botched opportunity. Likely they are delegated more than their fair share of menial chores around deer camp when they're young, but at least they have the opportunity to hunt and learn from their experienced elders year after year. Mesmerized by the old timers' stories, they dream of future deer hunts with their cousins, dads and, especially, their favorite uncles.

Johnny was a regular at our Fearless Leader's tavern during the highly regarded Thursday night pool league. An uncle – his "Uncle Wilho" who he describes as a "typical old Finn from the Iron Range" – had tutored him in shooting pool and the fine art of hunting the white-tailed deer.

Wilho is tall and stocky with an ample belly. Johnny looks up to his uncle both literally and figuratively. Reverting to his native language, the old man calls his favorite nephew "Jussi Poika" (Johnny Boy). After all, wasn't it Uncle Wilho who had taken the young Jussi Poika to Palo for Laskiainen, the Finnish sliding festival where they enjoyed the ice hockey tournaments and the curling bonspiels? Traveling even further northeast to Isabella, they laughed and cheered at the annual St. Urho's Day parade in honor of the legendary saint who drove the grasshoppers out of Finland and saved the wine crop. That was about as far away from home as Wilho traveled. The one exception was visits to Lake of the Woods for some serious mid-winter fishing. Those trips provided the key ingredient for burbot soup which, as was the old custom, was served with chunks of rye bread to relatives during January. And, of course, there was mulled red wine with black currant juice with which to wash it down. "Perhanan hyvää," utters Uncle Wilho, smacking his heavy lips, "Perhanan hyvää." (Damned good!)

Although he had a sister in Lantana, Florida, Wilho would not venture that far from his deer hunting grounds on the birch- and aspen-filled southern edge of the iron mining range. Big shouldered, he looked like he would be at home sawing the aspens in a lumber camp. He had, in fact, been a cook at such places in northern Minnesota and Michigan during his younger days. That was a while back.

Showing through the tattered sleeves of his ever-present flannel shirt were faded long johns. Red suspenders and the usual worn red "snot rag" were constant components of his year-round uniform. On his head was a weathered red railroad cap to match his tattered handkerchief. He blows his bulbous nose so often the other uncles accuse him of sounding like a locomotive. He liked the look of a railroad man. He is a simple man.

More often than not, liquid the color of motor oil trickles into his white whiskers from the corner of his mouth. Fond of Copenhagen – which he calls "Finnish candy" – he swears it brings him good luck when deer hunting. One cannot deny his success.

Sporting his salad-bowl haircut and playing an old family accordion, Uncle Wilho appears at the local VFW every Saturday night. Following a couple of straight snorts of brandy, the sweat flows from under his hair and down onto his chin, but it doesn't bother him, and he plays his heart out. The crowd polkas to his lively tunes that progressively deteriorate toward midnight, but no one complains. It's a typical Saturday night in the heart of the North Country where life is as sweet and as innocent as pure maple syrup.

Unlike Uncle Wilho, Johnny is the paragon of modern hunters. Not only is he equipped with the latest gadgets, but he also has the best gear available. Clearly, he is one of the most successful deer hunters and walleye fishermen I know. You see, Johnny is a competitor, sportsman, gentleman, executive and, did I say competitor? Many times he has made the difference between a pan full of plump walleyes or a can of Spam, which we carried on our Canadian trips in case of emergencies. The paint has nearly worn off of that old can.

At the outset of any of our frequent fishing trips, I would bet big bucks with anyone foolish enough to believe they could catch more walleyes than Johnny. Sure, there were times when one caught more than him by the time for shore lunch. But at the end of the day, it was Johnny's tally sheet that prevailed. You should have the picture by now, Johnny is one of those people you can count on to give 100 percent; some say it is 110 percent.

Tutored by Uncle Wilho, Johnny is also musically inclined, and he plays the electric keyboard in a popular fifties rock 'n' roll band on weekends and holidays. Not a Saturday morning couch potato, he is always engaged in some worthwhile endeavor. Like I said, he consistently gives 100 percent and has never been accused of anything less than total effort. Perfection is the standard to which he aspires. Cooking is an art to which he does not aspire.

Since Uncle Wilho had worked as a cook for a lumber company in his early days, he presides in the kitchen. Among his limited culinary specialties are hot pancakes for breakfast. He is adamant about the family hunting party coming to his house early in the morning before the hunt to be fed heartily. It's tradition, you know.

"You gotta have a good breakfast if you're a gonna hunt deer," Uncle Wilho confidently states in his heavy Finnish accent. "Ohukaiset (pancakes) tomorrow," announces the former lumberjack cook, and Johnny politely approves, as does the rest of the party. No use fighting it. But underneath their polite facade was a groan and tightening of the stomach muscles. You see, Uncle Wilho would get up in the middle of the night to begin fixing breakfast, and he swears that the secret to good pancakes is a red-hot cast iron griddle. But the deer hunters will tell you that his pancakes are unique because they defy the laws of physics. Being burned to a crisp on the outside, they remain runny on the inside. Heavy as the local iron ore, they remain lodged in the gullet all day.

While he tolerated pancakes for breakfast and would never complain or criticize, Johnny always dreaded the thought of another antacid morning. Nonetheless, Uncle Wilho was his mentor and had taught Johnny the ways of the whitetail. Patiently the old man advised him to watch does carefully since crafty old bucks would always follow the does for safety. Many fine bucks were harvested by waiting for the does and lesser bucks to pass to see what was tailing behind. It was sound advice from the venerable lumberman.

Following the morning drives, it was off to the individual deer stands. Everyone dispersed to his or her assigned areas, and the relaxing afternoon hunt began. Understand that Uncle Wilho was a walker and not a stander. His skinny legs did not look like they could support his ample belly, but he relished the long drives and never complained about walking. However, he did complain about the younger hunters perched in tree stands.

"You don't know vhere da hell dey go, but you gotta get in der vhere dey hide," he said at least a dozen times a day. "Ya don't get dem by loungin' in yer tree stands like a buncha' monkeys." He is a basic hardcore stalker. If stalkers are the princes of deer hunting, then Uncle Wilho was the unquestionable king.

In contrast to Uncle Wilho, Johnny likes to climb high into the trees where he is concealed from the constantly sniffing nostrils of the whitetails. There he revels in the beauty of the autumn woods and can see an expansive landscape through which he has established numerous shooting lanes. Smelling the forest and feeling the sun's warmth are among the luxuries of a sunny autumn deer hunt.

A couple of deer seasons back, one warm and sunny afternoon when no deer were moving, the forces of slumber began to appeal to Johnny. A caffeine or sugar fix may rescue one from such drowsiness, but why must one always fight the intoxicating and seductive allure on such a beautiful autumn day in the woods? He yawned.

Recalling the horror stories at his DNR hunter safety training, Johnny realized it is dangerous to remain in a tree stand when drowsy. Easing from his lofty perch, he made his way to a sunny southern exposure on the leaf-covered bank of the St. Louis River. It beckoned him to the rocky shore like the Lorelei.

Locating a site that would offer at least a half hour of welcome sunlight shining through the forest canopy, he carefully groomed a plot beneath an aging tree and leaned back. He yawned again. Soon his eyes peacefully glazed over and his head began to gently nod. The sun warmed his face, and the forest scents relaxed him and beckoned him to join forces with tranquility. Pressure and stress were foreign, meaningless words. Peaceful repose.

He hadn't abandoned his post like an AWOL sentry; he was merely cashing in on the luxury of the great outdoors, harvesting the forest's secret treasure. Drifting into the depths like a scuba diver into the murky boundaries of the unknown, he was entering the zone of darkness.

Sounds were selectively filtered out by the somnambulant sentry and did not interrupt his dive into darkness. He had earned this luxury. Consciousness flowed in and out like the ebb and flow of the sea. Tranquility base, the eagle is napping.

Not wanting to awaken with a start or to continue to nap, he intended to slowly ease back to consciousness like the rising of the harvest moon on a clear, still November night. Tales are often told of the buck of a lifetime heading for the hills after being spooked by the wakening movements of a careless napper. Johnny was too smart to make such a foolish mistake. Drifting toward alertness, he opened his eyes and methodically began to capture the essence of his surroundings. Rotating his head deliberately as his uncle had taught him, he scanned the surrounding territory while resting his thumb firmly on the rifle's safety. Upon completing the visual search to his satisfaction, he sat up, stretched and gathered his wits and basked in the glory of his successful doze. He felt proud and skillful, youthful and confident, sly and cunning. Glancing at his abandoned tree stand, he smiled. How lucky he was! The other members of the party had missed out on the precious bounty.

Making his way back to the cabin, he knew he was going to arrive later than usual. He hoped Uncle Wilho wouldn't focus those aging blue eyes on him and be the first to inquire about the afternoon's events. Such interrogations could be as thorough as a final exam. Over the years, Uncle Wilho would beam with the joy of seeing his favorite nephew bask in the lofty praises of the family hunting clan. Youth led from innocence and naivete to assume the role of dominant buck hunter

under the trusting but demanding tutelage of the alpha polka king himself.

"Vell Jussi Poika, vhy didn't ya shoot dat big buck?"

"What buck was that?" Gulp!

"Da one dat followed dat bunch of does dat vere a runnin' right toward yer stand."

"Well, actually I ..." He would have to choose his words carefully.

"Didn't ya see dat buck?"

"Well, no, I guess I …" He was in trouble.

"Ya saw da does, didn't ya? They vere headin' right fer ya, dey vere."

"Well, not really." Uncle Wilho was getting too close for comfort.

"Jussi, Jussi, Jussi Poika! Didn't ya see nothin' a'tall?"

"Nothing significant …" admitted Johnny, innocently. Indeed he had neither seen nor heard anything.

"Vell I'm not surprised Jussi Poika," chuckled Uncle Wilho as he spit snoose into an empty bean can and pulled his faded handkerchief from his pocket. "No vonder ya didn't see anythin'," he said, as he began to smile. "Vhen I got vithin a city block of yer stand, I heard ya a snorin'. Snorin' louder den an overloaded freight train."

Rattling up a Buck

It was getting toward the end of deer season and the party hunters were weary, like a hormone-driven buck at the tail end of the rut. Lifeless, pale weather blanketed the North Country, and snow flurries were in the forecast. Two precious tags remained unfilled – a buck tag and the bonus doe tag that was traditionally held in reserve until the last day. But what the party anticipated most was some relief from Uncle Wilho's infamous morning pancakes. They were ready to call it a successful season and go home.

"Ta day is da day!" exclaimed the old Helsinki native, trying to instill some enthusiasm into the troops as he always did as the season's end approached. He was rejuvenated after a late evening visit to the sauna.

"There are two things that are holy to old Finns," says Johnny Boy, "Church and sauna. But for Uncle Wilho, deer hunting ranks up there real close." One could sense it in the old man's voice when he spoke of deer.

"Ya never know vhere da hell dey go, but ta day … ta day ve're a gonna find 'em," predicted the old hunter.

The family deer party knew the old man would get a shot at

a buck on this day. No one could figure out how it happened, but he managed to bring one down every year at this time. Without a doubt, he would return to deer camp with that snuff-stained toothy grin, and the stories would once again flow. They could see it coming. It was a certainty.

"You monkeys gotta get outta dose trees and start walkin' an stalkin', dat's da secret," proclaimed the aging hunter. The usual chorus of groans arose from the troops. They had heard the story before; every year, in fact.

"Jussi Poika, you come vith me on dat stretch between da railroad and da river," said Uncle Wilho as he laced up his weather-beaten boots. "I can feel it in my bones; ta day ve're gonna git 'em down at da old Green Swamp. Da does ain't even gonna be safe. Ta day is da day."

"So, we'll take a doe today if we get a good shot instead of waiting till the last day?" asked Johnny.

"Ta day, if it's brown it's down," responded the old timer with a twinkle in his faded steel-blue eyes. His voice was laced with confidence.

Opening a new bottle of doe scent, the only modern hunting aid that he believed would work, Uncle Wilho accidentally spilled several drops on his right boot. The same Arctic Pac boots that the mice had eaten the liner out of during the past winter, thus causing a major delay on opening day. The stark aroma of doe urine filled the busy cabin.

"Be careful the bucks don't run over you when you lay down a scent trail as you're walking and stalking," quipped John's father with a grin. Laughter filled the room as the hunters paired up and departed for the morning hunt. Excitement always accompanies the troops as they leave the cabin.

Off they went, protégé and mentor. Nephew and uncle. Modern hunter and old schooler. Uncle Wilho never used a compass and didn't like tree stands. No grunt tubes or rattling horns would be found in his hunting arsenal. He only wanted the basics: gun, ammo, sandwich and a tin or two of "Finnish candy" for good luck.

At the beginning of the season they had observed whitetails matching up their antlers and sizing each other up. Uncle Wilho had long ago explained how deer rattled by testing their antlers against each other's. Later in the season, they would be bolder and clash their velvet-free antlers in true tests of strength. But he scoffed at those who carried antlers to imitate the rattling of fighting bucks. "A big vaste a time vhen ya could be a stalkin'," advised Uncle Wilho.

Through the thick hazel brush they walked as quietly as is possible in the infamous Green Swamp, an area so thick that Johnny had never seen a deer. They tried to stay in sight of each other, which was comparable to trying to walk through the brush quietly. After an hour or so of stalking, intermixed with rests and a refill of snoose, John was convinced they had somehow gotten turned around.

"Let's head over dis vay to vhere ve're meetin' da rest of 'em," said the mentor as he gestured to the north with his bare, leathery hand.

"Well, actually I don't think it's that way, Uncle Wilho. I think it's over there," John diplomatically said as he gestured in the direction he thought was the correct way to proceed. "I think the river is over here on our left."

"No it ain't," said his uncle with confidence. "You'll take us all da vay to Floodwood goin' dat vay." He knew his way around this stretch of hunting land. "It's right over dis vay, you'll see." And off he went with renewed energy. He would show Johnny that he was still in command.

John followed along but listened closely for sounds that would give away the location of Highway 2, which also happened to parallel the river. Crashing though the bush, he was glad to hear a distant drone of an eighteen-wheeler and suggested to Wilho that they stop for a minute to listen.

"I think if we listen closely we'll hear a grain truck on the highway, so the river has to be over there," John said as he checked his compass for corroboration. "I think we're right next to that slow current stretch where the mayflies come off like a snowstorm on warm nights in early June."

Stopping and listening, the old man eyed the cloudy sky and wiped his nose on his jacket sleeve. When he squinted, his eyes nearly disappeared in the wrinkles of his aging face and he asked, "Vhich vay did ya say da river vas, Jussi Poika?"

"Over to our left, I think," said Johnny, although he knew for sure that it was on his left. "Since we heard that truck on the highway, the river has to be over here on our left."

"Vell I'll be darned," said the old man, eyeing Johnny with more than a hint of indignation in his voice. He tipped his engineer's hat to the side, leaned against a scrawny aspen, and scratched a patch of whiskers that he had missed while shaving. "That damned river is on da vrong side! Vat da hell is it a doin' over dere?"

Somehow maintaining his composure, John alleged as he did not know how the river could have been so negligent. It was a moment that John remembered and treasured, but he wouldn't tell that one in deer camp. Uncle Wilho was his mentor.

Hiking in the direction of the St. Louis River, they turned west while keeping in sight of each other's blaze orange as best they could, and then meandered toward the spot where they would meet the rest of the party. They had spent more time finding their way than they did hunting. But the result was that they had circumvented much of the Green Swamp, thus arriving at the rendezvous point with time to spare.

Naturally, a family tree stand had been erected near the traditional meeting location. It had been put there for such occasions, and John suggested that he might as well climb up into the stand and hunt while they waited. On more than one occasion, the late arrivers had driven deer in the direction of the stand as they tramped toward the rendezvous. It was worth a try.

"I'll go over an' get up on dat birch stump by vhere da big blueberries grow in da spring," said Wilho grudgingly. He was not a monkey, he would not climb a tree stand, but he would stand on that old stump and watch for deer with the attention of a security guard.

Climbing into the tree stand, John was deeply disappointed that the best hours of the morning hunt had been wasted. Just out of sight, he knew the old man would be on the stump and hoped that he wouldn't blow his nose or drop the metal snoose can lid as he fidgeted while waiting for the troops to arrive. John began planning his afternoon hunt that would follow the morning fiasco as he scanned the thick hazel brush for movement.

Within minutes he sensed motion and nearly shook his head in disbelief as a respectable doe cautiously ambled across John's trail and moved in the general direction of Uncle Wilho. She stopped to nibble on a red-osier dogwood stem – a favorite deer food – then looked quickly over her shoulder. That gave John hope that a buck might be in pursuit. Waiting for the second deer can be disastrous if nothing follows and a choice deer was passed up. While the doe he had seen was respectable, perhaps the buck might wander close enough for a clean shot. Meanwhile, the doe occasionally stopped to nibble dogwood, then continued on toward Uncle Wilho.

Suddenly, the familiar sound of an aging Winchester shattered the quiet. John recognized it without question and smiled as the sound echoed throughout the river valley. Following the sound of the gunshot, he peered anxiously in the direction of Uncle Wilho for movement of a deer in quick retreat but saw nothing. As his gaze returned to the territory in front of his own stand, he froze at the sight of an alert basket-buck whose fearful eyes were also locked in the direction of Wilho, the deerslayer.

Satisfied that all was quiet after a few minutes hesitation, the buck lowered its head to the trail. Not the trail laid down by the interdigital glands between the hooves of the doe that had just passed, but the trail put down by Uncle Wilho's old boots. No sooner had the buck begun to wag its tail, as whitetails usually do before taking that first step after pausing, than John heard the metallic tinkle of a snoose can lid. It was followed shortly by a familiar sound of a certain Winchester – the same rifle that has duct tape wrapped around its battered stock. That sound was also familiar to John. It was the sound of Uncle Wilho trying to reload an old firearm that never received the proper care and cleaning it should get. The sound was that of a jammed gun and the fumbling old man's hands contributed. He never wore gloves unless it was well below zero. Metal on metal, brass and steel, clinkity-clink. Accompanying the metallic rattling were the grunts and a few unintelligible Finnish swear words from the stout man who was as old as his firearm.

Hearing the curious sounds, the buck again froze. Johnny held his breath and hoped for the opportunity for a shot. Minutes passed and a red squirrel chattered. Instead of bolting for the next country, the buck lifted his head from the scent trail and trotted eagerly in the direction of the rattling sounds coming from Uncle Wilho's birch stump. No buck should have responded to the sound of metallic rattling, or rattling of any kind, not that late in the season. It was a fatal mistake.

There would be stories around deer camp that night. Not stories of getting lost in the Green Swamp but of the virtues of a hot sauna, the value of a big pancake breakfast before the hunt and the advantages of not being a monkey up in a tree stand. Stories of how a helping of "Finnish candy" brought a double dose of good luck. Though no one would hear the whole incredible, improbable, yet true, story of how Uncle Wilho had unknowingly rattled up a buck.

Deer Camp After Hours

The nickel-dime games were winding down at Johnny's deer shack, and it was a good thing since the card players' ability to concentrate had drastically diminished while the rules were becoming more complicated. Hoyle would be dumfounded! Deer season was in full swing, but the hour was getting late. As usual!

"What was wild again?" asked F. D., the railroad engineer, as he examined his five tattered, sticky cards for the second time.

"Pay attention, jacks or better to open, trips to win, and one-eyed jacks are wild, as are the red deuces," responded Brewster, the bleary-eye dealer and deer camp regular. "How many do you want?"

"Gimme three cards, zoo-breath, and I'd prefer them off of the top of the deck this time," responded F. D. in jest.

So it went. The nightly duel was developing between those who wanted to play cards all night – generally known as the winners – and those who wanted to get some much-needed rest for the next day's deer hunt.

"Okay, just one more round of deals and then a final game of five-card showdown for a dollar. That's the tradition," proclaimed Brewster. Poker would last at least another half hour.

As the uneven kitchen table was finally cleared of cards, empty snack wrappers, and adult beverage containers, some of the inhabitants of the North Country cabin hung damp, smelly socks to partially dry during the night. Others crashed immediately. The Counselor was arranging gear for the morning hunt while Johnny brushed his teeth. F.D. rummaged through his faded Duluth Pack looking for the essential earplugs for the certain onslaught of nocturnal snoring.

Naturally, there is an official fire tender for the wood stove in the deer shack whose responsibility is to ignore all complaints about the heat or lack thereof.

"You are certainly welcome to sleep outside in the snow if the temperature is not to your liking," James admonished while showing his toothy Texas grin. "And don't let the door hit you in the behind on your way out."

"You're as cruel and cold hearted as a lawyer," related Jussi, as he stowed his topo maps away for the night. "Maybe I should have said heartless lawyer instead."

"Hey, Jussi Poika, Johnny Boy, how many cords of wood did you saw last night? I got two chainsaws at home, and I swear you snore louder than both of them." It was our Counselor's veiled attempt to divert the certain incoming flow of legal practitioner insults.

"Wasn't me snoring; it was F. D.," responded Johnny innocently.

"Baloney, the windows were rattling in that corner all night."

In that smoky corner of the cabin an air mattress was being inflated to help ease the pain of arthritis during the night. But the creative and arguably demented minds of deer camp produced an unending stream of jokes about various forms of inflatable objects, generally of the female persuasion. Most of which are not repeatable, else the guilty parties would be appropriately banned from any further participation in any organization or community activity in our small town.

The last of the tennis shoes and hunting boots had begun to thump on the creaky wooden floor when F.D. climbed into the top bunk of the wobbly bed that leaned radically toward the rustic wall, itself being less than vertical.

"Hope she holds up again for another night."

"You don't hope half as much as I do, F. D.," responded Big Gary, the occupant of the lower space. "Don't be floppin' around up there tonight."

Always present at deer camp is at least one bed that emits a shrill creaking sound with every movement. Nefarious comments are usually hurled toward the unlucky occupant. Did I say "usually?" I meant "always."

"What was that rhythmic squeaking we heard from your bed last night, Toothy?" asked Brewster.

"Forget the squeaking, I want to know what Ol' Toothy was moaning about," chimed in the Counselor.

Laughter fills the simple cabin, and there is danger of the festivities getting out of control and continuing deep into the frigid November night. But the troops had hunted hard, and as the crude comments gradually subsided, the lights were extinguished.

"Hey, wait a minute, turn it back on a second!" exclaimed the railroad man.

That pattern seems to occur just about every night.

Zippers sounded as sleeping bags were prepared and eyeglasses were stowed in the final seconds of light. Invariably, a flashlight would still illuminate the darkness for a few minutes by someone who was shrewd enough to keep a light within reach during deer camp.

When darkness finally floods the room, the noise level may quickly subside – or more likely – resume only after a brief pause. The silence lasts about 20 seconds.

"Good night, John Boy!" smirked someone in the darkness.

"Night!"

"Hey, John Boy, where are we hunting tomorrow?" asked Big Gary, his brother-in-law.

"Maybe Uncle Wilho's favorite spot down by the Green Swamp where he rattled up that buck, then the Honey Hole in the afternoon. Or maybe the other way around."

"I like that idea. Are you with us, Doc?"

"The Doctor is in. Are we going down that trail that you marked with that big red flag?"

"Big Red? Hey John!" exclaimed Big Gary as he sat back up in bed. "Remember Big Red, that girl you went with when you played with the rock 'n' roll band? That one with the big wazoos. I remember your mother really frowning and saying, 'I didn't think too much of that girl.' And you said with a straight face, 'maybe not, but dad sure liked her.' Remember that?"

"That was pretty funny all right! Anybody set an alarm to get up in the morning? Counselor?"

"Yeah, I set mine for noon. Now shut the heck up and get some sleep."

As the cold northwest wind gently stirred the naked trees next to the darkened cabin, the quiet was once more interrupted.

"Hey, Toothy, what's the weather for tomorrow?" asked F. D.

No response came.

"Is ol' Toothy asleep already?"

"That grinning Texan is either asleep or else he overdosed on the habanero sauce – or was it napalm – that he dumped in that pot of venison chili." said Brewster.

"I think the weather is gonna be okay tomorrow. I don't think it's supposed to snow," continues F. D. "You know … that reminds me of a Snow White joke."

"Oh no! Not again!" moaned the Counselor. "Can't somebody shut him up?"

Once the deer camp inhabitants start down the bad joke path it's hard to stop. Previous to this point, the comments and jokes were at least half-decent and relevant. Now they all had one thing in common, they were degenerating exponentially in crudeness.

"Well, I've got the all-time tasteless joke," began F. D. excitedly.

"We're supposed to be surprised?" chuckled the Counselor. "You of all people!"

"What has 10,000 legs but can't walk?"

"I give up." Offered Brewster after a few seconds of silence.

"Jerry's kids!"

"Get that animal out of here," bellowed the Counselor. "How can any of us sleep tonight with a sick mind like that loose under the same roof?"

"How about the one where the girl asked her dad if she could use the car?" continued F.D. without hesitating. He was on a roll.

"No! Don't you dare tell that pathetic joke. You degenerate!"

"And the dad said ..."

"Someone shut that pervert up," shouted our honorable member of the Bar.

The activity level had resurged.

Quick to jump back into the fray, Johnny asks, "Anybody have a good lawyer joke?"

"Lawyer joke? Isn't that redundant, mister ambulance chaser?" questions F. D. who couldn't wait to stir things up again.

"Don't go there," warns the Counselor. "Don't get me started! Just don't get me started!"

"Does anyone know what animal leaves a trail of slime as it moves across the ground?" It was Ol' Toothy, the re-awakened Texan.

"A lawyer, I presume. Very funny! Now go to sleep," begged

our beloved Counselor.

"I got it! How do you tell if your lawyer is lying to you?" Without waiting for a response F. D. immediately blurted out, "His lips are moving! Ain't it great!"

"How original," groaned our legal beagle. "You should be on television."

"And here's a goodnight kiss for you, Counselor," shouted F. D., farting loudly as he is frequently prone to do during deer camp.

"Better check your shorts after that one, you turkey choker," said the Counselor laughingly. "You're a sick, sick man!" He is used to the verbal abuse after hunting and fishing with the group for so many years. But he has a strong Irish heritage and is wiry like a terrier. Often he is called upon to adjudicate a dispute over whose buck will score more points or which walleye is heaviest. In spite of the verbal abuse, he is patient with us and has no trouble defending himself, especially after a few snorts of good Irish whiskey.

Laughter eventually subsided and the comments waned. Some of the deer hunters approached sleep, but even then any activity can result in a response, like the person in the squeaky bed turning over.

"Hey, no teepee creeping over there in the corner." It was F. D., of course.

Only a couple of muffled responses resulted, and quiet swiftly returned to the tired deer hunting party. They were winding down at last.

Without fail, someone will get out of bed during the dark hours. According to the Counselor who was raised with seven brothers and sisters, one can tell whether the nighttime wanderer is from a large family or an only child.

"The only child guy makes a lot of noise when he takes off his boots, opens the fridge during the night or goes outside for a biological break. He isn't used to thinking about waking anyone, but those of us who grew up with a lot of siblings learned to be quiet the hard way. We got the snot kicked out of us if we woke anyone during the night."

The Counselor's theory makes a lot of sense, but one is cautioned against trying to apply too much logic to the behavior demonstrated during deer camp. It is a time of merriment, absurdity and companionship. A time for practical jokes and playing cards and plotting against the awesome whitetail. A time to get out of life's fatal ruts and perhaps to fulfill a distant primordial hunting urge. Who knows? Does it really matter?

Outside of the dark, rustic cabin, the night air cools rapidly and the wild animals that are not afraid of the dark roam freely. They are aware of the audible clatter and deer camp stench emitted from the shack and undoubtedly give it a wide berth. But they are safe for the time being. Probably more secure than those who are residing within the hallowed walls of deer camp ... after hours.

Deer Camp Cook

If one were asked to paint a picture of the camp cook, his palette would likely be overflowing, and the resulting portrait would not be one of beauty. Our resident culinarian at Johnny's deer shack can be a tough customer; he earned a black belt in martial arts and teaches kickboxing. But that is not the reason we try to appease him.

We stopped for breakfast at a family restaurant on the highway heading due north from Duluth to our simple but picturesque deer camp. It was to be our last store-bought meal for a week.

"Better order a good meal, boys. This is the last chance we'll have to get any good chow for the next seven long days," advised the taunting F.D. as he eyed the menu.

"Yeah! And it may be the **only** meal you'll get for the next seven days," grinned our camp cook. It had already begun but would change once we arrived at deer camp and lunchtime approached.

He is not the kind of guy one would ordinarily picture as a deer camp cook. His conservative haircut and boyish face seem consistent with his erect posture and well-trimmed moustache.

Considerate, mild mannered and polite, he has eyes that are deep brown and sensitive. Hardly the picture of the cantankerous, cigar smoking, unshaven, beer-bellied stew burner with a dirty apron who gets up in the morning and stabs himself a couple times with a dull and rusty kitchen knife just to get in the mood to cook. But he is by no means wimpy, either. He is confident, to be sure, but not macho. Standing well over six feet, he is in great shape and quick witted. And the man can cook!

While many deer camp cooks grudgingly tolerate cooking, he actually enjoys his chores and goes about his duties with military precision. Planning the meals, buying supplies and the never-ending cleanup takes considerable time away from his deer hunting. He never complains.

The youngest of seven kids, he watched his mother cook and, since that chore occupied most of the time in her day, he helped. Later he became a short-order cook and still shares in meal preparations at home. We are talking major interest and experience in cooking.

During a stint in the Navy as a metal molder, he learned the politics of the "cumshaw system." That is, he was known to have roasted turkeys in the blast furnaces for other sailors in exchange for things his group needed. He knows the importance of keeping communications open and the value of getting along with others. We understand this concept, too.

Now we are not talking about fancy-pantsy cuisine like fricasseed hummingbird tongues in a Parisian Café or similarly presumptuous culinary extravaganzas. We're talking hot, hearty grub at deer camp when it's 10 degrees outside.

Getting up early each day of deer camp, he begins his chores in the morning quietly and is careful not to rattle and bang pots and pans. Soon, wafting through the stale cabin air comes the sweet, smoky scent of bacon lazily sizzling in his legendary cast iron skillet. Mingling with that tantalizing smell is the bold aroma of freshly brewed Colombian coffee from a slow-gurgling, old-fashioned pot. Hunters begin to arise from their bunks having been unknowingly awakened by their alerted salivary glands. No one has to be called for breakfast.

When he opens the oven door; the scrumptious smell of freshly baked buttermilk biscuits spills luxuriously into the cabin. Oh, Lordy! Pass the butter and honey! It will soon be dripping off of your little finger as you devour the morning feast. Breakfast, lunch and dinner; he always delivers, rain or shine.

Being an avid duck hunter, he has been known to surprise us with an elegant roast duck stuffed with wild rice and morel mushrooms. What better culinary representatives are there of the North Country? Actually, wild rice is not a member of the rice family; biologically speaking it's a grass family member that thrives in shallow waters of rivers and lakes in the Great Lakes region. Preferring slow-moving currents, its grain ripens around late August. It has been harvested for centuries by Native Americans in the region. Once you've tasted the nutty flavor and crunchy texture it's easy to understand why they fought to protect their ricing waters. No wild game dinner is complete without wild rice.

A perfect compliment to wild rice dishes are the rich morel mushrooms he preserves by air drying after collecting them in the spring. Looking like a sponge, or like a "corn cob" according to Uncle Wilho, the mushroom's ridged caps are hollow from top to bottom. They range in color from nearly white to almost black but are usually yellowish-gray to brown. Finding them is not too difficult if one looks in sandy or limey soils in old apple orchards or areas with lots of dead elm trees, especially in regions that get a lot of snow. However, their habitat range is broad, and specific locations are kept as secret as blueberry patches and hot fishing holes. Deer love to eat mushrooms, so they must be good!

Our chef shines equally well during autumn Canadian fishing trips when he peels the bark off a dead birch log and soon has a roaring, aromatic fire ready for shore lunch on even the coolest and wettest of days. Golden brown lake trout fillets that one can soon smell clear across the lake come out of his hot skillet. "I'm the kind of guy that always likes to release his fish …" he says with his boyish grin, "into a pan of 175-degree cooking oil." The scrumptious fillets are accompanied with simmering fried potatoes that are well browned and crunchy when you eat them. Mixed into the spuds is a generous helping of deliciously mild onions. A little salt and pepper and one's mouth simply waters at the aroma. Even a lowly can of baked beans is turned into good chow with a couple shots of hot pepper sauce. Man, the savory shore lunch spread could serve as a model for a Norman Rockwell painting. To die for!

Being an arguably intelligent bunch of addicted deer hunters and trout fishermen, we realize the value of having such a member in our illustrious group. While we would not actually go so far as to tell him how much we appreciate his efforts, we have learned not to criticize his culinary prowess. One must be careful during such outdoor adventures not to raise the ire of the cook lest he decide to abdicate his position and leave us to our own devices. That would mean certain death by food poisoning or starvation.

Why risk losing all that we have by launching snide remarks or hurling negative culinary insults at this generous, likeable man? Sure, he can handle the criticism; he is a plant manager who worked his way up the corporate ladder, as did most of the troops. But he is the group's only good cook. We are sensitive to the situation. We love the guy's cooking and hope the heck he'll continue for a long time. So when the opportunity presents itself, we are united. When our resident chef places a plate of unusually overcooked eggs before us and apologetically says, "I'm really sorry, but they're overdone and some of the toast is pretty dark." Our response is swift, unified and emphatic as we all shout:

"**Great!** That's **just** the way we like it."

Alone in the Woods?

Moving with caution and attempting to remain as quiet as possible, Johnny eased out of the familiar pickup seat and glanced at his illuminated watch dial. Zero-dark 30. He had arrived well ahead of schedule and was pleased with himself as he gathered his gear in preparation for the dreaded solitary trek to his secluded tree stand. It was the opening morning of deer season in the North Country. And it can be scary when darkness prevails and you're alone in the woods.

Shouldering his rifle sling, he groped for the flashlight he had equipped with a red lens and fresh alkaline battery. Nudging his body against the truck's door and extinguishing the dome light, he stood quietly to allow his eyes to adjust to the darkness and admired the distant stars still visible in the sky.

His thoughts returned to earth in an instant as the eerie sound commenced. Low at first, rising gradually in volume and tone, and then falling again. Other voices joined in the chorus as the remote northern forest sprang to life with the haunting and mysterious howl of the northern timber wolf. The hair on the back of John's neck stood as erect and rigid as a military sentry at Arlington National Cemetery. Sure, he had heard the sound before, many times as he was growing up in northern Minnesota. But one never feels complacent when the call of wolves echoes throughout the North Country in the darkness – and you realize that you are not alone.

Standing in silent awe, he recollected a visit to the tree stand earlier that spring when he was making some necessary repairs and had observed an enormous black bear. He had experienced genuine fear that time, for lying at the base of his tree was his weather-faded Duluth Pack containing his two peanut butter and jelly sandwiches, a big, juicy pickle and a slice of Claudia's chocolate decadence. When hungry bears are fresh out of hibernation the pickings can be slim, so they will eat just about anything, including a person's lunch. Clutched tightly in Johnny's hand was his wooden-handled claw hammer. The big bruin could have his lunch, but he vowed not to remain in the elevated stand after dark. He'd attempt to smack him right between his beady little eyes if he had to, but he was not staying alone in the woods after dark. Easing his grip as the bear ambled away without evidence of having caught his scent, or the scent of his lunch, John sprinted back to his truck while making frequent nervous glances back to the trail.

Trips to a deer stand during spring are normally pleasant and relaxing. Making deer stand repairs and modifications, or clearing new shooting lanes, can be performed at the same time that morel mushrooms emerge. It is an annual event for Johnny when the woods are awakening from the long North County winter. Pockets of white trillium carpet the floor of the rich woods where he hunts. Occasionally, he finds a trout lily with its yellow petals and mottled basal leaves. It has always been Johnny's favorite, and what a great name for a spring wildflower.

Painted trillium emerges during spring in the nearby acid bogs where tamaracks grow and where smart old white-tailed bucks hide when the pressure is on during deer season. Later on in the bogs, delicate orchids like the showy lady's slipper and moccasin flower blossom. Following the orchids are the strange sundew plants that derive nitrogen, lacking in their habitat, from the insects they snare and digest.

Marsh marigolds, or cowslips as some call them, decorate the northern swamps and brooksides with their deep yellow flowers shaped like buttercups, only larger. Spring is a time when red-winged blackbirds perch on last year's cattails and proclaim their territories, and spring peepers sing their joyful love invitations. And best of all, the pesky mosquitoes and vicious black flies are not the scourge on these spring visits that they will become during those long summer months preceding deer season.

His mind returned from recollections of spring and refocused on the dark morning. He tried to convince himself that there were other animals in the woods that howl besides wolves.

Last year as he sat in the same stand on opening day of deer season, a crafty lone coyote stopped to examine one of Johnny's plastic film canisters containing fresh doe-in-estrous scent. Sniffing the odor deeply and testing the air, he moved from location to location along Johnny's scent trail and eventually approached within 10 feet of the tree in which Johnny was perched. Though knowing he was not in any imminent danger, apprehension rose as the coyote approached closer and closer until Johnny finally shouted, "Hey, get the hell out of here!"

Scampering away in an erratic manner, the coyote escaped to safety with his tail between his legs while looking around in a ridiculous attempt to spot the source of the verbal command. This comic recollection did not erase the present anguish as Johnny stood next to his truck in the clear, nippy air listening to the haunting wolves. One never forgets the fretful emotions on dark and dreary mornings during deer season.

Opening the truck's door to activate the dome light, he welcomed the illumination like an old friend. Instead of waiting to get to his tree stand to load his high-powered rifle, he placed a shell in the chamber and inserted the five-shell clip into position. Since he had arrived early, he took advantage of the opportunity and waited for several extra minutes before traipsing cautiously and anxiously toward his stand. As he drifted into the darkness, he thought of similar situations in the woods.

Often he had experienced close encounters with animals that posed no threat of danger. A wandering ruffed grouse, scampering red squirrels or flitting chickadees were always welcome distractions that kept his senses sharp. But when an adult great-horned owl landed thirty feet from his tree stand early one spooky November morning and began bobbing his head up-and-down and side-to-side while staring at him as if he were fresh meat, Johnny felt a hint of fear. He was the vulnerable hunted instead of the fearless hunter. It was an uncommon, unpleasant perspective.

"Risk and vulnerability are no strangers," Johnny once said. He had spent a couple years in Washington, D.C., swimming with the sharks on Capitol Hill. "Is there anything in the woods more dangerous than that?" he asks in all seriousness. He seems to thrive on adversity. Though traveling extensively with his job, he always managed his calendar judiciously so that he would not miss the deer season opener. Never!

Another time while hunting by himself three years ago in a lonely stretch of woods near Grand Rapids, Johnny ascended into his tree stand and had just gotten settled when bits of organic material started to rain down on him, and he heard loud crunching and chewing sounds. Thinking it was a squirrel, even though it was still nearly dark, he gazed up in the higher branches of the tree and spotted a big porcupine. So just what do you do when you find out that you are sharing a tree stand with a porky? Although it startled Johnny at first, he recalled a similar incident when he felt the tree stand ladder vibrating. He looked down to see a bristling porky climbing up. Now that's a predicament!

"I had to take some decisive action on that one!" said Johnny with a laugh. "I started dropping stuff on his head and he got the message real quick and retreated. I never knew they could move so fast. And I can assure you that I didn't have any trouble staying awake in the stand that morning."

Once on a clear November morning when he stumbled toward his deer stand after a long night of poker, he witnessed the explosive takeoff of a ruffed grouse right from under his boots.

"It makes the old heart pound and makes you feel kind of jittery for a long time," says Johnny. "Those events start to make you a little paranoid about the forest critters when you're in the woods – and darkness makes it worse."

His mind had been occupied all day – from the time he left the truck and walked toward his stand in the darkness until late afternoon. Then another buck wandered into Johnny's rifle range as one had done during each of the previous three opening days of deer season. "Why is it always late in the afternoon when I get 'em?" questioned Johnny.

Sure enough, long and dreary afternoon shadows covered Johnny as he worked to clean the six-pointer. Crouching with his arms covered with deer blood up to his elbows, he again thought about the wolves, the lone coyote and one huge black bear. Standing up, he hoisted his rifle and made sure it contained a round of ammunition in the chamber in case he had to fire a warning shot to scare something off. That gave him a little comfort. Leaning the deer gun against a nearby maple tree, he scanned his surroundings thoroughly in the quiet and darkening woods before he stooped and returned to his bloody task.

He realized that the threat of any real danger was extremely remote, although he knew that one of the animals would eventually smell a meal and investigate. Something would come to devour the steaming viscera under the cover of night. Knowing that would happen created some concern since he still had to drag the buck out by himself during the fading twilight. And as he did, he felt that occasional perplexing and uncomfortable anxiety that one experiences when they are in the woods in the dark. It was the stark realization that when you are alone in the woods – you are not ...**alone** in the woods.

Sport Shop Payoff

Hunting and fishing opportunities are extensive and diverse in the North Country. Equally diverse are the people who live there. You will not find clones in this part of the country. No, they all have personalities, and many are unforgettable characters.

Reciting "10, 11, 12," she placed the individual piscatorial peons into my yellow and white minnow bucket. It always drives me nuts when a dozen minnows, and only a dozen, are counted out one at a time. Besides, I was a good customer at the Fearless Leader's sport shop.

"So, anything else you need today, Doc?" she asked. Her voice was hard; her whole life had been hard.

"That will do it," I replied as I leaned on the cluttered sport shop counter and looked her directly in the eyes. "By the way, have you been keeping out of trouble for a change?"

"You're a rotten son-of-a-gun," she snapped. "And I ain't sayin'." Turning her head away, she put her hand to her mouth in an effort to hide a smile but her eyes gave her away. She could take a little ribbing as well as she could dish it out. "You're rotten!" she repeated, "just plain rotten."

One of a kind, she was one of the more colorful sport shop employees! About mid-to-late 60s I would guess, but then I am not a good judge of age. Having spent many years outdoors, the sun and wind had ganged up to weather her long, plain face. Her graying blond hair was short and straight, and her clothes were slightly masculine. She could be abrupt and tough like a street fighter, but she was helpful to her customers. Her dark, sad and fading eyes came to life when she verbally sparred with me. We both enjoyed such interchanges.

"Going fishin', Doc?" she asked as she moved toward the cash register with the plastic minnow bucket.

"No, just picking up a few appetizers for dinner," I responded in jest.

"You get out of town, you rotten so-and-so," she said with a partially controlled cackling laugh that was repeated three or four times. Smothering the smile again, she wiped it away with her hand. "You're rotten, rotten, rotten."

"Going deer huntin' this year?" I asked earnestly.

"Oh geez, I don't do much deer huntin' anymore. Although I'll probably take my grandson out a couple days during the week. Too many kooks out there during the weekend!" she answered. Her concern was real; it was visible in her eyes.

She had gone through the predictable deer hunter's cycle. When one is young, it's impossible to get enough hunting, and it's the amount of game taken that's important. Then it seems one develops more interest in matching wits with trophy bucks. Later on in life, hunters desire to turn their interests toward conservation and preserving our hunting heritage. These hunters are satisfied with watching deer or even feeding them. I like the concept of predictable cycles in nature.

"I spend more time grouse huntin' now," she said. "My dog likes to do that, she does. We just go for a drive and she smells them. No foolin'. She starts gettin' birdy, and I just stop the car and we check out what's going on. I really just go huntin' because she wants to go. But the grandson likes to hunt deer; he does like to do that. So I'll just take him out sometime during the week," she said. "So, you stoppin' over at the tavern? I'm about to close up, and I'm going to go have a tap myself."

Enjoying a beer in the evenings with her close friends at the Fearless Leader's "tav-ern" – adjacent to the sport shop – was where I usually saw her. Preferring tap beer to bottled, she sipped her beer, smoked and socialized for hours. For many folks, that is the normal thing to do in the small towns that dot the map of the North Country. Everyone seemed to know what everyone else was doing – but at least they cared.

She wasn't a regular member of most community activities, but if there was something special going on around town, she was there. A few years back, a special spearfishing season was allowed for Native Americans on our local lake. Having bought a can of beer for the road, she and a girlfriend went to see if anything out of the ordinary was going to happen. Trouble had been expected, and our nervous little town was full of assorted state and federal authorities. Unfortunately, one of the law officers motioned for her to stop her vehicle. Both of the occupants' beers were stuffed under her pickup seat. That was good for an "open container" violation, and that was when I started asking her routinely if she was staying out of trouble. She laughs about it now.

Yes, she was a plain, yet colorful character. I am glad that I had the opportunity to get to know her. I am likewise glad that she took her dog on special hunts and that she was willing to take her grandson deer hunting and share her love of the North Country with him.

By the way, I also took the opportunity to buy her a "tap" every time I saw her at the tavern. And, after a year or so, the minnow count changed. It became swift and generous – often very generous – although I never seemed to get around to mentioning that fact to the Fearless Leader.

Brewster the Mooseter

According to his count, he had attended 28 different schools by the time he finally finished high school. It wasn't as though he was a bad student or anything; he was an "Army brat" who had grown up early and learned to be tough. He was about to learn that a moose could be pretty tough as well.

Although he had lived in many countries including Japan, Germany, Norway and Denmark, and in big cites such as Washington, D.C., and Paris, it was the outdoors that interested him most.

"I decided to become a wrangler at the tender age of 17," asserted Brewster with a proud smile, "so I left home for Colorado and pursued a career outdoors."

Wrangling was tough work, but he loved riding horses on the open range and even advanced to the rodeo where he learned bull riding. In the Big Sky Country with its abundant wildlife, he also acquired some secrets of successful big game hunting and got to be a darned good guide. After serving his military obligation in the 101st Airborne and then putting himself through college, he began a forestry career in Wyoming. That kept him in the field where he wanted to be.

Managing forest land suited him just dandy, and his knowledge and common sense approach were soon recognized. Having conducted promising field research on aspen growth, his work led to an attractive job offer in Northern Minnesota. It was an easy transition for him, and he soon settled into the job and into the traditions of the North Country. Not only did he love deer hunting, he also sought to know the other flora and fauna of the region.

Discovering the secrets of harvesting wild rice by traditional methods and learning where to find the tiny – but tart and tasty – wild blueberries that grew in acidic soils were favorite pastimes.

Judiciously, he discerned how to locate and observe sharp-tailed grouse strutting on their open grassland booming grounds early in the spring. Stomping their little feathered legs rhythmically on the ground, the nimble game birds race around in circles sputtering and cooing. How different than the ruffed grouse that lives in the forest and is the most widely distributed resident game bird in the country. Selecting special logs within the forest, the male ruffed grouse advertises his availability by "drumming" his wings rapidly in a manner that sounds like a small gas engine starting. Brewster admired the fact that the ruffed grouse survives better in a forest with variable aged aspen, like those managed for timber production. The two grouse species are so alike, yet so different. So are foresters and forest preservationists.

Acquiring knowledge and experience in the forest industry, he became involved in controversial forest practice and policy issues like logging in the Boundary Waters Canoe Area. That involvement eventually led him to St. Paul to work on balancing the state's policy on forest management with the interests of the environmental community. Some called him a "loggy-ist" since he represented the forest products industry. Of bull riding and lobbying, he said, "Both are equally dangerous professions if you're not careful." Naturally, we told him that our assessment of his change from the rodeo to the capitol was that he was transformed from a bull rider to a bull shitter. Be that as it may, he retained his love of the outdoors and for big game hunting.

A few years back, Brewster and a friend applied for a Wyoming moose permit. They decided if either one of them got a license; they were going moose hunting together. Both would enjoy the company and also appreciate sharing in the backbreaking job of taking proper care of a 1000-pound animal and packing out the delicious meat.

"The fun of moose hunting is definitely over the instant he hits the ground. I guarantee that," advised Brewster. He knew what he was getting into.

Loading up the half-ton pickup and hitching a trailer to ferry their nimble Jeep brought sweat to the successful applicants' foreheads. For the first week of November temperatures were exceptionally high, and Brewster's wife, Jan, decided to tag along to take advantage of the summer-like climate to be outdoors. She also took a good book along for company. She knew what

she was getting into, as well.

His hunting buddy had a contact – a foreman at a local garage – who had been in touch with some of the guides that had flown over the region to spot hunting opportunities. Armed with their reconnaissance reports, the trio headed for the hills with high spirits. Such is the case on the first day of any hunt. But nothing worked in their favor except that Jan got a lot of reading accomplished while she waited as the guys hunted the game trails and wetlands.

That night they met the garage foreman at the local watering hole and, like field marshals plotting the next attack, discussed alternative approaches. They plotted late into the night.

Early the next morning, off they went. Taking a rough gravel road far into the foothills, they passed a couple quaint ranches that had seen many snows and hunting seasons. Unloading the Jeep, they headed up a narrow rocky trail southwest of Jackson Hole. The men split up and hunted in different directions, only to return at lunch without any sign of moose. After the hungry hunters devoured lunch, they moved higher in elevation.

Arriving at a high mountain stream, they discovered a 100-acre dense willow thicket. Each took up a position near the outer edge of the wet area and moved slowly downstream. Brewster blew his birch bark megaphone-shaped moose call. It looked promising.

About that time, a well-used pickup truck approached Jan who was reading alone, but contented. Coming to a halt, out of the truck climbed two gray-haired but able-bodied women who issued greetings. They lived at nearby ranches and, despite the heat, were dressed in faded blue jeans and men's flannel shirts as they started out on their way to hunt mule deer. Concerned that Jan was lost, or otherwise needed some assistance, they soon discovered that they shared the same interest in the author whose book Jan was reading. An opportunity opened to further discuss books, the warm weather, and hunting.

Meanwhile, like its prehistoric relatives, the dark bull moose slunk in the shadows and grazed quietly in the willows. It was gigantic and sported a respectable rack to boot. Seeing the big animal at 300 yards, Brewster quickly assessed the situation. If successful, they would be able to get the Jeep to the site. Nearby was a sturdy cottonwood, so a come-along anchored to the tree would make the loading job easy. It was the perfect setup.

However, since the moose displayed his rump toward him, Brewster had to wait for a better chance, which he did with strained but knowledgeable patience. Eventually, the moose paused and looked back over his shoulder. It was all the opportunity that Brewster needed. The moose dropped in his tracks like a quarter-ton of frozen steaks. Bingo!

While removing the spent shell from the breech so he could reload, Brewster glanced up to observe his moose. Shocked, he saw him up on all fours and heading downstream. No! He fired his rifle a second time.

Across the mountain meadow another shot rang out as his partner spied the rambling animal and took his turn at hurling lead in its direction. The monster did not go down but kept moving ... at a quicker pace.

In the interim, the women's conversation stopped, and all eyes were gazing in the general direction of the three shots.

"I wonder if they got my moose?" queried Jan. "It sure sounds like it."

But before either ranch lady could answer, another two gunshots pierced the thin mountain air.

On went the wounded moose. Only later did Brewster learn that a wounded moose may go into shock and just start walking as long as possible. By now the moose was leaving the security of the sparse trees, as well as the primitive trail, far behind.

Upon hearing the second volley of shots, Jan again spoke, "I hope they got it this time. Surely they did!"

A half mile and two additional shots later, the moose weakened as he bled out, stumbled and went down for the last time. The hunters found themselves in a situation where they could not even access the bull with the versatile Jeep. The fun was indeed over!

Following the final series of gunshots that rang out, quiet finally returned to the hillside, and Jan said, "Well, that's got to be it. Thank goodness! I've been looking forward to having some fresh moose meat. Sounds like I'm going to have me a nice big moose rump roast."

"Well, I have to tell you," began the older of the two ranch ladies as she removed her western hat and mopped her damp forehead, "after all that shootin' out there, it sounds to me like about all you're going to be having is moose burgers."

Cellulite and Lace

Hunting for deer in the North Country is more than a lame justification for tramping off into hallowed forests each fall.

Deer hunting is tradition. During deer season many young hunters are excused from school for a whole week with a simple handwritten note from their parents. For it is a time when parents and their kids, accompanied by cousins and uncles, gather sustenance for the winter as many generations before have done. Others hunt with old friends or business associates instead of family. However, they all rejoice in a time of fellowship, reliving memorable hunts, and reviving youthful enthusiasm. But for one unique person in the North Country, it was a time when the traditional buck hunters became the hunted.

"Hey, Doc, put a couple dollars in the juke box! Don't be a cheapskate!" Coming from the kitchen of the tavern was her hearty shout, "Woo Hoo!"

Her voice was unmistakable! She loved to hear the jukebox blare, and she possessed a grand voice that enabled her to sing along with the latest country and western ballads that she knew by heart. I couldn't carry a tune in a bucket, so to me her golden voice sounded like a successful recording star's. And as each poignant tune ended, a booming "Woo Hoo!" emanated in an elevated decibel level directly proportional to her affection for the song. It was her own personal and measurable signal of happiness.

She was one of those exceptional characters of the North Country. Her lips were full and melancholy, and her favorite lipstick – whenever she used it – was a brilliant red. The crimson color transferred to the tips of her cigarettes and the rim of her whiskey-filled drink. Working there part time, she also enjoyed socializing at Jackson's Bar which was located just down the highway a piece from our Fearless Leader's fabled "tav-ern."

Divorced for as long as I had known her, she had learned to be assertive and uninhibited, to put it mildly. She often tended bar on weekends when the place was busy, although she actually preferred working in the kitchen where she made a scrumptious pepperoni pizza. She loved to eat. Loved to shake the dice at the bar for a round of drinks as she periodically scanned the field of local patrons through her Coke-bottle glasses. Observant and quick-witted, she always had a good joke to tell that was usually risqué. When she was so inclined, she could swear like the saltiest of seasoned sailors. However, her 24-carat heart was as significant as her frame. She was one of my all-time North Country favorites.

"So, how do you like my new hair color, Doc?" She had asked casually one day as deer season approached. "It's pretty dark! I think the color of that bottle of hair dye was called 'Hillbilly Black'. Woo Hoo!"

A solid woman, she had arms that were husky. Once, she had hugged me around the neck at a wild surprise birthday party, and I thought I'd pass out before she loosened her firm grip. She had worked hard all her life, and the loose skin and dark circles under her eyes were a testament to long years of labor. Working so hard she had, in my opinion, deserved the right to party hard.

Seeing her glide around the small wooden dance floor without effort, I was surprised and envious of her gracefulness. She swayed to the music and, with great joy, shouted an occasional, "Woo Hoo!" This was no junior-high cotillion. Well, when she twirled around the dance floor one Saturday night as a popular local country band was playing, a brief hike of the big girl's skirt revealed an accidental glimpse of generous cellulite thighs and appealing black lace. A memorable sight.

The next day during a rare break from her busy kitchen routine, we both sat at the bar while munching on a bowl of leftover popcorn. She commented, "Geez! Deer huntin' is only three weeks from tomorrow. You going out this year, Doc?"

"You betcha!" I quickly responded. "I wouldn't miss opening weekend of deer season for anything nowadays. Do you ever go huntin' at all?"

"Oh, hell yes!" she replied while focusing her moist brown eyes on me with intensity. "Only I do all of my huntin' right in here in the Great Indoors. I don't have to go out there in the cold like youse guys. There's plenty of horns right in here during orange week when all the guys come up from all over the Midwest," she giggled heartily and lustily while throwing her head back.

"And you know what, Doc?" she asked with an ornery twinkle showing in her eyes behind the thick and heavy eyeglasses. "Only twenty-two more days until I bag me a buck! Woo Hoo!"

The Gentle Warrior

The phone rang at my rustic log cabin a month before deer season. As soon as I answered, I knew something was wrong. His voice quivering, the Fearless Leader spoke in a hushed tone. The news was not good. The Gentle Warrior had died.

I had always suspected the old guy would fall through the last ice of the season or tumble out of his small fishing boat and drown when he was alone. He was too old to climb up and fall out of a tree stand, but I am sure that he would not have minded going that way. But his heart just plain gave out ... and my heart was heavy.

I admired the old guy, and I can still picture him in my mind. His flat-top was gray and his mechanic's uniform green. Wind and rain had darkened his skin like fine-tooled rawhide, and on his face were deep furrows instead of wrinkles. Distant were his eyes. Otherwise, his face was innocent and his upper lip was prominent and stiff. Our Fearless Leader had shown me an old yellowed newspaper clipping reporting that 30 gallons of moonshine had been discovered, but they did not apprehend the actual distiller. I wouldn't have guessed that it was the same quiet old man.

Seated at the end of the bar, always on the same stool, he generally avoided direct eye contact but still managed to survey the sights and sounds of the locals. Hard of hearing – so he always said – he could still overhear hunting stories, and he could tell you who had taken the largest buck in the county. When fishermen were having a beer and discussing where crappie were biting, his long, distinct ears always perked up like an alert buck. But his hearing failed abysmally when his wife, who surpassed him in height, girth, and resoluteness, gave him his marching orders.

"She still keeps a tight line on him, Doc," the Fearless Leader had advised me. "He can't get away with much like he used to in the old days when he was a hell raiser."

As a young buck, he had hunted and fished all over the North Country. It was clear that he passed his love of the outdoors on to his son, our Fearless Leader. Also passed on in his genes was the same stiff-legged walk, and perhaps some of his penchant for mischief, although both of these traits have been denied by our esteemed Captain.

In the years before I moved to the North Country, the deer hunting party was divided into two teams, and the Gentle Warrior had directed one of them. He stuck up for his team. Arguing with the other captain, he made sure his team had only their fair share of tough drives like the infamous "Pump Handle". When other parties tried to move in on the Gentle Warrior's hunting grounds, he drove them away like a dominant buck protecting his territory.

"Dad was quite the hunter in those days," the Fearless Leader recalled. "He was tough, but he was fair to everyone."

As time passed, the old man's stamina decreased and his judgment became clouded. Age brings a man's senses down as surely as a timber wolf downs an ailing buck. He had borrowed the Fearless Leader's pickup and put it through the ice by being the last one to fish for pike during the spring.

"Son-of-a-gun wouldn't take his own truck out on the thin ice; he had to borrow mine," mumbled the Fearless Leader.

Besides that, there was the time he trudged into the tavern anxious to show off what he had bagged from his favorite duck blind on the Upper St. Croix River early that morning.

"Damndest goose I ever saw!" he exclaimed with a look of puzzlement as he proudly displayed a federally-protected mute swan.

"That one was a real humdinger!" recalled our Fearless Leader. "I thought he was going to jail over that deal."

Another time he marched into the busy restaurant toward noon with a bobcat over his shoulder.

"Oh no, Dad! You need a permit to keep one of those," exclaimed the horrified Fearless Leader.

"What the hell do I need a permit to keep him for?" asked the puzzled old man. "He's dead now!"

It took a lot of delicate negotiating with the DNR to settle that situation. Nonetheless, the mounted bobcat can still be seen today residing over the Gentle Warrior's end of the old wooden bar.

Continuing to hunt as he aged, he shot one of his best bucks a couple years ago when he was 82 years old. Last year, using a forked branch to support his ancient 20-gauge, he managed to take a plump doe on opening day. When the word was passed down the line of hunters, cheers went up as if he had killed the biggest buck in the entire North Country. Everyone enjoyed seeing the old man succeed, and I suspected that we harbored hopes of emulating him. But when the old man tried to unload his gun and banged the butt of the stock repeatedly on a pickup's tailgate with his cold hands stiffened by arthritis, the troops either ran over to help him or scattered like a frightened covey of quail.

Past his prime, he had relinquished his position to the younger bucks. No longer in charge, he sat in his vehicle and watched with solemn eyes as the Fearless Leader directed the troops. Sharing coffee with his hunting buddy between drives, he rested in the warmth of the pickup. When he stared into the woods, I'd like to think that he relived memorable hunts of days gone by and battles he had won. He was one of my favorites.

I'll never forget the day I shot my first buck with the Fearless Leader's hunting party, a 10 pointer. Squatting on the ground next to the buck, my knees were still quivering. It was also my first hunt with the Fearless Leader's gang. Grinning like a school kid with a perfect report card, I heard the old man and others approach.

"I've got to give Doc a pat on the back," the old man said as his big hand – the one with the finger missing – reached over and pounded me on the back. As he congratulated me, I had the sense that I had officially been accepted into the hunting party. It was a grand feeling, a feeling of elation and belonging. Not only had I taken the biggest buck of the hunt, but also I had been accepted. I shall always treasure that magical November day in the North Country.

Later that evening, after the deer had been checked at the DNR station, our weary band of deer hunters reassembled at the Fearless Leader's "tav-ern." Having earned the day's bragging rights – meaning the opportunity to buy a round of drinks for the troops – my new hunting party raised their glasses to toast my success. I was hooked on deer hunting forever. After another round, the Gentle Warrior surprised everyone by taking out his wrinkled wallet, which he seldom did, and ordering another round of drinks for the party. I felt honored. Not everyone did, for he became the focus of an intense glare from his wife. Trouble was brewing.

"You don't have any business buying a round of drinks," admonished his wife. "It's time to be getting ready for church anyway." Her voice was stern; her word was the law.

The old rascal paused for a tense moment as the troops

looked at him for a response. What would the old-timer say? Would he buy the round or not?

"I ain't a goin' to church tonight," he finally declared in an assertive and confident voice. A hush fell over our end of the bar. Had we heard him right?

"And I ain't a goin' to church tomorrow either," he proclaimed much to our shock. "Tomorrow I'm a goin' huntin' again with the boys."

Everyone held his or her breath as the boss of the family stalked out of the tavern. The quiet old fellow still had the courage to stand his ground like a dominant buck. I was awestruck! Maybe that's when I started referring to the old gentleman as the Gentle Warrior.

Now one may not be able to prove with absolute scientific certainty that there is a Promised Land, but I'd like to believe so. For if there is, then there is no doubt in my mind that deer hunting is allowed. I just hope that the good Lord doesn't expect the Gentle Warrior to be paying attention in church on Sunday morning during deer season.

They All Look
Alike in the Woods

Lining up for the day's first deer drive on a crisp, clear November morning was cause for excitement. Eagerness and exhilaration could be felt in the cold air as everyone prepared for the drive in his or her own way. We were a disparate group of hunters, to be sure. However, dressed in our blaze-orange hunting garb, we all looked alike in the woods.

One of the party regulars was a bartender employed at the Fearless Leader's well-known "tav-ern." Stout, strong and quick behind the old wooden bar, she was a confident and assertive person. Perhaps aggressive is the better word. She had always been pleasant to me and had once invited me into her home for venison chili after I hunted a nearby tract of county land.

However, she could become less than tactful after a couple of beers or a stressful day behind the bar. In fact, she was known to go toe-to-toe with the Fearless Leader on a regular basis. Few did. Not a wishy-washy person; she made it clear where she stood on any issue. Her will was as hard as an antler and she could be as strident as a dominant buck during the rut. That's why Cammie had rightfully earned the name "Kamikaze."

Now Kamikaze liked nothing better than to harvest the

biggest buck of the season, then tease and taunt our Fearless Leader or any other male hunter unmercifully. As a member of the tavern's softball team, she had plenty of opportunities to remind the guys of her trophy bucks throughout the summer. She seemed to enjoy seeing them cringe with embarrassment in front of the visiting teams. She could really dish it out.

November had once again returned to the North Country, and we all followed our Fearless Leader in search of our beloved white-tailed deer. A whole new season; a whole new ball game, so to speak.

At a particular site known as the "Half-a-Drive," the troops marched single file down an old logging trail nearly reclaimed by advancing birch and aspens. As we spread out along the trail and maintained visual contact, there was a luxurious period of idleness before the abbreviated drive commenced. Younger hunters spread out on the snow or practiced shouldering their firearms and scoping imaginary 12 pointers sneaking through the dense patches of new growth.

While feasting on venison jerky or candy bars, we patiently waited for vehicles to post standers and trucks to be safely parked. The pickup drivers then had to position themselves before the hunt began, so we had plenty of extra time. Time to enjoy.

As we relaxed and savored the bright morning, we awaited the signal to commence the march through the familiar parcel of land. Feeling the effects of my morning coffee, and perhaps a twinge of jitters since gunfire usually accompanies the Half-a-Drive, I yielded to the call of nature. Anointing a nearby birch stump, I was like a wolf marking his home territory. As I finished and cautiously zipped the fly of each layer of clothing with my cold hands, I realized I had just performed my biological break in plain sight of Kamikaze. Oops! In a line of drivers all dressed in bright blaze orange everyone had looked alike.

After completing a successful drive – Avis had dropped a

forky – I approached Cammie in embarrassment to tell her that I wasn't thinking who was next to me before I relieved myself.

"Was that you, Doc?" she responded while unscrewing the top of her thermos as she sat on the tailgate of her truck and waited for Avis to dress the buck. "Not a problem! I've seen you guys do it plenty of times before, but I didn't realize it was you," she said with a broad smile. An impish look of satisfaction spread over her face as she continued, "No big deal … to me, they all look alike in the woods."

The Greater Fool Theory

His friends often call him "Bear" and at times, it is a fitting name for our Fearless Leader's only son.

Bear was born with Down's syndrome, and his parents had the foresight, intelligence and courage to give Bear all the opportunities they gave to their two daughters. Working in the Fearless Leader's restaurant just like the rest of the family, Bear washed a lot of dishes. Over the years the whole family contributed patiently to Bear's growth and development. He evolved into one of the most friendly, popular and recognizable residents of our tiny North Country community southeast of Superior.

"Fish on! Fish on!" shouts the legendary Moose Rider each and every time that he enters the Fearless Leader's eating establishment.

"Fith on! Fith on!" comes Bear's happy reply from the kitchen. They are the best of friends.

As a student in our small town's schools, Bear participated just like everyone else, although he received special skills training because his learning rate was different than the other students'. With the support of a lot of special folks the Bear continued in school, and when he was generously awarded a high school diploma it was a tremendous occasion.

The local crowd, packed into the school's homey but warm gymnasium, conversed about the weather, fishing and the fact that Bear was among the small but distinguished list of graduates. Proud and dignified as a Rhodes Scholar, Bear strolled across the stage and energetically shook hands with the school principal and superintendent. It was an emotional, heart-warming event. Because never before, nor since, has anyone received such a rousing, sustained standing ovation during high school graduation in our little town. There were many tears.

Now the Bear has a hearty and enthusiastic handshake, but he is far fonder of hugs. Bear hugs, to be exact. And he never cared much at all for just shaking hands with the ladies, especially the attractive young ladies.

It is interesting, and perhaps somewhat intimidating, to note that he is not the least bit inhibited around women the way so many of us are. While vacationing in Hawaii every spring, he has to be closely watched. Otherwise, he will approach a large group of bikini-clad ladies and strike up an innocent, friendly conversation. These discussions may lead to the Fearless Leader shelling out big bucks for rounds of expensive poolside drinks decorated with pineapple slices and pink umbrellas. They were compliments of the Bear ... kind of. Tactfully, the Fearless Leader comes to the rescue and digs deep in his pockets and enjoys the conversation – and the scenery, too. The Bear beams. Mrs. Fearless Leader is not amused.

The Bear has also been included in many of our infamous hunting and fishing trips. Traveling to the Dakotas, Michigan's UP, Ontario and Manitoba, he adds a lot of excitement to the excursions. One can count on that.

Bear does not like to get up early in the morning to go fishing or hunting. Nor does he like missing breakfast. Consequently, he doesn't go often. He does accompany the Fearless Leader and Moose Rider when they canoe our favorite spring-fed trout stream on opening day in search of brookies. However, Bear prefers fishing for crappie and sunfish from the comforts of the family pontoon boat, which also holds more tasty snacks and treats than any canoe.

When it comes to deer hunting, Bear is not nearly as dedicated. Three years back he accompanied the Fearless Leader's troops just before Thanksgiving. Bear was simply not having fun. Can't say the rest of us were, either. The day was one of below-zero temperatures and a biting northwest wind. The weather wasn't pretty, but the troops' spouses were all gathering at Mrs. Fearless Leader's house for holiday baking. Therefore, the Bear was strongly encouraged to go hunting instead of staying at home. He loves cookies. And brownies. Man, does he ever!

Our Fearless Leader stood with Bear in a small, wooded ravine on the first deer drive of the bitter November morning. Standing is not a favorite tactic of the Fearless Leader; driving through the bush is not a favorite pastime of the Bear. He did not carry a loaded firearm, of course, but he was a valued member of the hunting party. Although "party" is perhaps a poor word choice when the weather is brutal and whitetails are scarce in the North Country.

After the second unsuccessful drive, Bear's wide forehead was furrowed and his thick glasses rode low on his red, runny nose. He looked miserable.

Suddenly, before the next drive could be planned, the Fearless Leader became downright vocal and agitated about something. Shoving his .30-06 into its case and banging the truck door, he was engaged in a heated one-way discussion with Bear, who sat in the cab with his head hanging low. The words were not pleasant. The Fearless Leader stomped toward us with a glare on his face as we poured luke-warm coffee and cupped our hands around the mugs for warmth.

"Doggone him! I told him to go to the bathroom before we left. Now he's crapped his pants so I've gotta take him home."

"Hey! No problem," we said. What else could the Fearless Leader do in that situation?

"You're the brains here, Doc. Go ahead and arrange the next drive. Take the "Heartbreak Drive" off of County Road A, and I should be back by the time you're done," said the Fearless Leader over his shoulder as he turned toward his truck. His renowned dimples were absent.

He tramped back to his pickup, and slammed the door again. Starting the cold truck, he gunned the engine and spun the big tires in the crunchy snow. He was pissed! The Bear sat motionless, his head down. Then he pushed his thick glasses back in place with a stubby finger and appeared to sigh. It was a long, deep sigh.

We watched while stamping our frozen feet and shivering as the Fearless Leader backed his truck, turned around and drove past us on the logging trail leading to the paved road. And as the

truck roared past, Bear rotated his head in my direction, and I could see his face through the frosty truck's window. If I hadn't known better, I could have sworn that I saw him smile.

I kept thinking about his smile as we finished the challenging Heartbreak Drive. We were cold and tired. No deer sightings were reported, no shots fired. The wind had increased, and the wind chill dipped as the sky clouded over. Enthusiasm plummeted.

Since I had lost my ride, I trudged over to one of the other hunter's trucks and climbed in. The seat was cold, but at least I was out of the penetrating winter wind.

"Got any coffee or hot chocolate?" I asked hopefully. "My thermos is in the Fearless Leader's truck."

"Yep!" he said as he poured the remaining contents of his thermos. "It didn't last long today, Doctor. Colder than heck out there. A brass monkey wouldn't have a chance on a day like this."

"Windy, too." I added. "No buck in his right mind would be roaming around the woods in this kind of weather. Then again, the same goes for intelligent buck hunters."

"For sure," he said as his breath began to fog the windshield. "Too darned bad about the Bear."

"Yeah, poor guy. He's not real big on deer hunting to start with. Not even when the weather's nice."

Sitting in the truck, we wiped our noses, removed our gloves, and shivered. He shared his nearly frozen chocolate chip cookies.

"By the way, did you happen to see the look on the Bear's face when they passed by?" I asked.

"No, why?"

"Well, never mind." I said. "I wonder what he's doing now?" I added, attempting to initiate a conversation to pass the time.

"Geez, come to think of it, he's probably hugged each of the gals two or three times by now, at least."

"Right!" I chuckled. "No doubt about it, that little rascal."

"More than likely he's finished off the remains of their pot of chili, and the last of the finger food is gone for sure. Scarfed!"

"You got that right. And if I know him, he's had at least a half-dozen warm cookies right out of the oven. Probably sipping on his hot chocolate, too," said I.

"Son-of-a-gun will probably be lying on the living room couch and watching the football game on TV at one o'clock," he mumbled as he handed me another frigid cookie. "And chomping on hot buttered popcorn or something, I suppose."

"That is, if he isn't curled up with the dog and taking a nice long snooze in front of the fireplace." I concluded.

"Right! That lucky dog."

We finished our luke-warm coffee and rubbed our hands. The truck's heater was beginning to exude warm air but it did not brighten our spirits.

"You know," I said with some reluctance. "Have you ever heard of something called the Greater Fool Theory?"

"Greater Fool Theory? Is that a new rock band or what?"

"No! Never mind," I said. "Never mind."

That was the end of the conversation. Naked tree limbs were undulating like waves while we listened to the brutal wind and waited for the Fearless Leader's return. My nose kept running and my feet were cold. We did not hear gunfire in the gloomy forest. We did not see any signs of deer. We were getting skunked.

Just past noon, the Great One, bringing his trusty pickup to a sliding stop, jumped out and hurried over to us.

"Did you get any on the Heartbreak Drive?" he asked without hesitation.

"Nothing!"

"Didn't anybody get a shot at anything?" he inquired with visible concern.

"Nope, didn't see anything at all," said my partner.

"Well, shoot! I'm really sorry guys," said our Fearless Leader as he pulled his hat down over his ears. "I told Bear to be sure to go to the bathroom before we left home. I hate to get mad at him, and I hate to screw up the deer drives like that, but after he made a mess in his pants, I didn't have any choice. I had to take him home. Sometimes he acts like such a fool."

"Right, you had to take him home," I replied as I wiped my sore, runny nose on the sleeve of my hunting jacket and shivered. "You didn't have a choice, and he's probably still laughing at the Greater Fools right now."

"Greater what?" asked our Fearless Leader with an inquisitive expression on his face. "Is that a new TV series or what?"

"Never mind," says I. "Never mind."

The Lure of Decoys

Hunters beware! There are decoys out there in the inviting autumn woods that may test the limits of one's self control. You may be surprised to hear who falls for the old decoy trick.

Some of them are television stars! Smiling wardens proudly parade their new white-tailed deer decoys across the television screen on Saturday mornings. Christened with clever felonious names like "Patsy" and "Buster," they have invaded the sports magazines and local newspapers, as well as the local Lions and Eagles luncheons. Deluxe models are even equipped with turning heads and wagging tails operated by remote control to tempt one further while driving favorite back roads when amorous bucks are on the move. So beware, my friends!

"Looks like the real thing when you're driving by one," warns the head of our renowned hunting group. He often is called "Our Fearless Leader" by the troops, especially when chaos prevails. That's most of the time when the days become shorter and the leaves turn color.

The approaching deer season seemed like an appropriate occasion to invite a conservation officer for an annual hunting safety speech. It's hard for service club program chairmen in the

North Country to attract exciting luncheon speakers whose services are free. As the midday presentation proceeded, heavy eyes glazed over and balding heads bobbed. Not the Fearless Leader, though. He was squirming in his folding chair when the downstate warden went on to jokingly describe situations where some hunters had been busted during recent deer seasons. Merrily he recited the names of a couple of highly ethical hunters – local boys – who had unfortunately been ticketed for some extremely petty offenses. Some were even present and accounted for at the gathering. As the luncheon concluded, some local folks, including the legendary Fearless Leader, felt offended by the thoughtless humiliation of the deerslayers in public.

Now I know that our regional warden of 27 years would not have been that vicious. Usually, he was a reasonable kind of guy. While he was not an active member of our local service clubs, he was rumored to have helped pull some strings so that the residents of our nearby penal institution could volunteer to clean smelt for the local Lions Club smelt fry hosted at our Fearless Leader's "tav-ern." Help that was much appreciated.

He also promoted the local community in which he lived. It was his home base while patrolling a huge district in northwestern Wisconsin for the DNR. "And remember, you guys, that I don't set the DNR's policies," he frequently reminded us. "I just have to enforce them whether I agree with them or not. And you gotta admit that I've always been fair."

Fair? Where on earth did we ever come to believe that things are supposed be fair? My executive assistant had once said, "There are only three situations where one could expect things to be fair. County Fair, State Fair and World's Fair!" That about sums it up in the real world.

Now our Fearless Leader understood where our local warden was coming from, but he didn't like the brashness of the visiting conservation officer whose reputation had already spread across the state. He was not universally respected within his own ranks. However, the thing that really set the Fearless Leader off is the DNR's practice of swarming around a car of hunters as they stop at isolated county road intersections in the North Country. Doors are suddenly jerked open by the boys-in-green, and rifle cases are quickly confiscated to determine if they are completely zipped closed or if the guns are loaded. Your favorite family heirloom may soon become a DNR auction item in this cheese-producing state if the zipper is opened less than an inch. In fact, two of the followers of the Fearless Leader lost their smoke poles a few years back because their cases were not completely closed.

"Just how is a guy gonna shoot at a deer with an unloaded muzzleloader even if the zipper isn't completely closed?" asks the Fearless Leader.

That incident still bothers the Fearless Leader. He's a man who has a lot of common sense and strongly believes in justice and equal application of the law.

"What's good for the goose is good ... to cook it low and slow," recites our leader, but we all know what he means.

"Buster," the DNR's prized 10-point buck, had once tempted the Fearless Leader for a fleeting instant as we enjoyed a lazy autumn afternoon ride in his pickup down County Road S during bow season. The massive antler spread immediately caught his watchful eye. About that time the video camera planted across the road did too. Oh the wonders of modern technology! Well, I'll be danged if several handmade cardboard signs didn't suddenly appear up and down the roadside which read "Deer decoy ahead."

"Didn't do it, no siree," claims the Fearless Leader who was rumored to have authored the warning. I can vouch for his innocence – which is indeed rare – because his printing is much neater than the poor penmanship that produced the makeshift decoy warning signs. Trust me on that one.

The Fearless Leader and I chuckled again as we discussed the cardboard posters. After six days of hard hunting in the last week, activity was waning and, as hunters often do, we passed the afternoon reminiscing about memorable pursuits. We chatted about hunting the Dakotas for pheasant and ducks, whitetails in Michigan's UP and our Ontario moose hunt. There were many hunts to relive, and the conversation continued until inky darkness enveloped our beloved North Country. Deer season was growing short. A time to reminisce; a time to plan.

Morning had already broken when the Fearless Leader arrived 35 minutes later than the previous day. His tardiness always increased as the final days of deer season approached, but he was smiling, and the dimples were once again showing as he brought the pickup to a halt in the snowy driveway. He didn't say anything, but the look on his face reminded me of a schoolboy with a slingshot in his back pocket. Something was up! His gun case reposed on the dashboard of the weathered pickup enclosing his trusty ought-six. Though everything seemed normal, that old uneasy feeling returned to my stomach as he engaged the clutch and we headed for the woods. Another Plan B?

None of the other members of our celebrated hunting party were out and about. The CB radio emitted a constant stream of static. The Captain and I enjoyed another respite from the lengthy unproductive drives through foot-deep crusted snow. We had meat for the winter, plus lots of pepperoni for our spring walleye trips. Traveling leisurely and carefree through the old haunts was indeed relaxing. Recalling the deer decoy sign incident, we both chuckled again. "That was a good one, Doc," proclaimed the Fearless Leader with a broad grin. "Gonna be hard to top that one."

We toured the heaviest hunted areas while watching the roadside for fresh tracks of a wily survivor, a tactic that often brought surprising results. It was a peaceful and untroubled afternoon. Lazy, in fact! But as we came to a halt at the intersection of County Roads A and S, all heck broke loose.

"Yeeeoooowww!" shouted the Fearless Leader as the pickup's

doors were yanked open. I froze. Reaching toward the dashboard in a flash was none other than the discourteous CO from downstate. The long arm of the law seized hold of the butt end of the Fearless Leader's gunstock which protruded at least four inches out of the end of the unzipped camo case. Yikes! How could that have happened? Our Fearless Leader knew better than that!

The expression on the arrogant warden's face immediately registered that confident and demeaning "I gotcha" look. I couldn't believe that our Fearless Leader had been so careless! We were busted!

Above the icy rustling of the wind-blown red oak leaves skidding across the crusty surface of the snow, above the noise of the idling engines of the stationary vehicles, and even above the clamor of the blue jays watching the tense scene arose a sharp peal ... an explosive peal of laughter. Fits of laughter climaxed in near hysteria as the warden withdrew the gunstock ... and only a simple wooden gun stock from the camo case.

"Gotcha!" shouted our exuberant Fearless Leader. "How does it feel to fall for the old decoy trick?" roared the Fearless Leader. "Wait till they hear about this one down at the Lions Club!"

Let me tell you a little secret, my friends, one that I can tell you from first-hand deer hunting experience in the scenic North Country. The boys-in-green don't think it's nearly as funny when they are the ones lured into the decoys.

Bear-Claw Donuts

What an expansive range of attributes people use to describe the wily black bear! From a cuddly fur ball inspiring the creation of the Teddy Bear, to a demonic, bloodthirsty man eater. Though perhaps not well understood, bears are awesome creatures. So when he decided on that once-in-a-lifetime hunt, he chose to go for a bear with a bow and arrow ... and donuts.

No stranger to bears, he had photographed lots of them at close range, real close. Deep in the Minnesota woods not far from Duluth, he and a fellow photographer enticed bears out of the dank swamps with bakery goods. Classified officially as an omnivore, the diet of bears is about 90 percent vegetarian, though they will, in fact, devour just about anything. He can attest to that. Acquiring a dozen slightly outdated packages of chicken from a grocer, the duo tempted the bears with the plump fryers. But after four scorching days in the hot sun, the chicken feast was partially cooked and alive with wiggling maggots, and it masked the rotten-egg smell of the paper mill not far away.

"We gotta get that stinking mess out of here. It's got to be keeping the bears from coming in," said his companion trying not to breathe deeply. "I'll bring a shovel tomorrow and bury it or something. That is, if I don't gag to death."

But before he had the opportunity to do anything with the putrid pile, the bears gobbled it up during the night, every last maggot. Yuck!

Scarfing down bakery goods – like bear-claw donuts and outdated tubs of donut glaze – fiercely appeals to a bear's voracious appetite and insatiable sweet tooth. Seemingly, bears came from miles around to join in the donut feast. Although the bears didn't get them all, for the local bakery was a legend in the North Country, and the photographers munched down about as many day-old bear-claw donuts as the bruins. Waiting for hours at a time for photographic opportunities, they sat in the back of the pickup with their camera gear. Covered by a topper and shielded from view with a shroud of camo netting, they were in donut heaven.

An incredible fact about bears is that one rarely hears them approaching through the woods, even the 300 pounders. It's the red squirrels and blue jays that announce the arrival of the big bruins. If grubs and ants happen to be on the bear's mind, one may hear the unmistakable sound of bark being ripped off of downed logs. It's conceivable that one could hear a donut-bound bruin smacking his lips in anticipation. Otherwise, they will drift into view silent as an evening shadow.

He also knew that although looking portly and being closely related to the pig, a big bear could run over 30 miles an hour. He had verified that fact when he surprised one grazing on grasses next to a county road near Esko. They traveled side-by-side for a quarter mile at 32 miles per hour according to the truck's speedometer.

"That's exactly the reason I invite you along on these photo shoots," his athletic young friend remarked with a grin. "When you're shootin' pictures of bears, the only thing you have to worry about is outrunnin' the slowest photographer … and that would be you."

Existing in colors not too different than Labrador retrievers, bears are primarily black, blond or cinnamon. Some have a splash of white on their chest. And smart? The bruins are the undisputed king of campsite robbers. They quickly recognize that a Coleman cooler or Duluth Pack usually means a free lunch.

Unfortunately, a problem arises when you match an intelligent and shy animal with some of the stupid humans who want to experience a Kodak moment in a place like Yellowstone. When people don't treat them as wild animals, the bears lose every time, since it is a lot easier to relocate or eradicate bears than it is to educate or control stupid people. Thus, fewer are seen these days at Yellowstone. Fewer bears that is, there is still an overabundance of stupid people!

About a half million bears survive primarily by staying out of sight. Unfortunate is the bear that discovers the easy pickings of garbage cans, or even worse, garbage can owners who think it's cute to feed the bears.

"A fed bear is a dead bear," according to the DNR folks. It's the truth!

Applying for a bear license is painless; waiting for three years to get drawn is not. Having experience with bears, he decided on giving them a "sporting chance" and opted for a bow hunt. That would require getting past the bear's tremendous sense of smell and within 25 yards. With the help of a legendary local guide, they established six baiting stations that they later reduced to three, due to inactivity or coyotes getting into the bait.

Hunting bears is similar to photographing them. Put out donuts, in come bears. First, one digs a hole or fills a barrel with goodies, especially bear-claw donuts. Next, cover the donut cache with logs. By cutting the logs to known lengths, one can accurately determine the size of a bear when one is not thinking logically, like when staring down the arrow at old Ursus at 25 yards.

It's pretty clear when a bear hits the site since they have the strength to scatter logs to uncover the donuts. Tied to one of the logs is a timing device that trips when old Teddy moves the log. With luck, a pattern can be established, a pattern that hopefully occurs during legal hunting hours.

The Swamp Angels site was the first baiting station established, and it had the best record of daylight hits, although it was also a popular hunting spot for whitetails and grouse during the autumn. There are berries there, too, as the bears can attest. Standing on his hind legs when he was spooked during a blueberry-picking trip, the huge bear was clearly a shooter. Henceforth, he would be known as the Monarch of the Swamp, in the same manner that crafty old bucks are given special names.

Another site was located directly across the lake from his cabin and back about 100 yards beyond a spring hole, one of many that fed the lake. Regular hits occurred there, too. A bear even left visible teeth marks when it chomped the ladder of his tree stand. Like a baby, a bear puts just about everything in its mouth, presumably to see if it can be eaten.

The lake site looked promising until two days before the opener when an incredible seven inches of rain fell overnight. Driving his fishing boat to the site to replenish the bait – after 15 minutes of bailing rain water out of the boat – he pulled the drain plug. The remaining water began to neatly drain as the boat was underway. But moisture had gotten into the gas tank during the rainstorm, and half way across the lake the five-horse sputtered and died. Frantically, he searched for the drain plug as water reversed its flow and started to fill the boat. Plugged up again and rowing to shore, he found the landscape completely flooded and so foreign that he could not locate the landmarks that led to his tree stand. When he finally got oriented, he discovered that the water was so high that the whole bait station was submerged. Abandoning the site, he got lost trying to return to his boat and had to listen for the sounds of cars on the highway to get his bearings. Not a good prelude to the hunting opener.

Located a half-mile west of the cabin was the old county dump. Although it had been closed, a bear was rumored to have returned on occasion. That's not surprising since bears are creatures of habit. How unappealing, though, to hunt at an abandoned dump for such a magnificent animal. He decided against hunting there at least for the time being. If things looked bleak later on in the season, then perhaps he would.

Working overtime at his downtown office, he got home late and received a phone call from the guide suggesting that he come over to see the bear a young hunter had harvested at the Swamp Angels. Though disappointed, he was relieved that it wasn't the Monarch of the Swamp. So, he continued to go back in search of him.

Sweeping across Lake Superior, the strong wind from the northwest prompted him to use a bottle of anise oil to spread the smell of licorice across the landscape. It should attract bears for miles. And that's exactly what happened. Sitting in his stand and constantly scanning the countryside as the branches reeled in the wind, he was shaken when a bear's snout arose out of the dense ferns and lowland vegetation 50 feet away and audibly sniffed the air. Catching his scent, the bear high-tailed it so fast that it was too risky to take a shot, and he watched in disappointment and disgust as the bruin, the Monarch of the Swamp, scampered safely away.

During that same week, another hunter who was working with the guide, and who was unhappy with his hunting site, had requested another location. So they all met at the tavern and discussed options. The other hunter chose the dump. He decided to stay with the Monarch and was encouraged one evening when he heard the familiar sound of bark being repeatedly ripped away as a bear searched for crawly snacks. However, the promising sound was shortly overshadowed by the blast from a high-powered rifle that echoed throughout the entire river valley. Clearly, it came from the direction of the dump. Afterward, he learned that a 350-pound boar had been taken. Determination was waning, but he stuck to the plan.

Continuing to bait the Swamp Angels site and picking wood ticks off of himself daily, he also expanded his number of hunting locations after the water receded from the site across the lake. Luckily, something began to visit the baiting station, so he headed that way on Saturday morning. Decked out in his hunting camo, he attracted the attention of a group of folks partying on a pontoon boat, and they began to follow him. So he had to play a waiting game until they were no longer curious or amused. In haste, he beached the fishing boat, covered it with camo material, and sneaked off to his hunting station. His timing couldn't have been worse, for a bear was already feasting on donuts at the site. He couldn't reach his stand or get close enough for a shot, and the bear soon vanished.

With the encouragement of having seen a bear, he returned to the lake site early the next morning, committed to spending the entire day. He nearly did. But a little luck developed when a dark shadow moved. Silently and cautiously his bear ambled into range. Finally!

Comparing its length to the known length of the logs, he was again heartbroken. While it was larger than the 80-pound bear taken earlier by the young hunter, he would not take a bear that small. Instead, he drew the bow and aimed at the bear's vital spot to determine how it felt. It felt a lot like buck fever. However, one's imagination can spawn a lot of negative scenarios that begin with an angry bear 25 yards away with an arrow sticking in its rump. Add a sugar buzz from chomping bear-claw donuts all day, and one can imagine the intensity of emotion.

Fall was descending upon the North Country, and brilliant colors and frosty nights prevailed. There was a sense of urgency in the air. The end of the baiting period of the bear hunting season was fast approaching. After the next weekend, he would have to ambush a bear if was going to get one, and that seemed far less likely than luring one into range with sugary bait.

Armed with a fresh supply of donuts, and facing gusty winds off of the big lake, he literally decorated the forest on Wednesday afternoon by hanging sweet morsels on low-hanging tree branches to help disperse their scrumptious scent across the river valley. While he didn't see the Monarch, the donuts were eaten by the time he returned on Thursday.

Repeating the performance, he distributed the donuts again on Friday. Wearily sitting in his tree stand Friday evening, he committed to hunting the weekend, although he had brought three days of work from the office, and the yard had to be mowed, hopefully for the last time of the year.

However, his planning came to a screeching halt as he spied a dark object that, with a little imagination, appeared to be a bear's head looking back toward his own trail. His heart began to pound, and his breath was stolen away. Experiencing that old, familiar feeling, he knew that the bear was going to follow the scent directly across the open space in front of him. He would have to gather his wits for the shot. Fortunately, he had the benefit of a practice aim at a bear with his bow. Looking away from the bear for an instant, he fought to gain control and to slow the surging adrenaline. When he looked up, the bear had disappeared.

Loading the surrounding tree limbs with the remaining sweets, even leaving a glazed donut on a small broken branch at the base of his tree, he left dejected. Losing his enthusiasm because of the string of bad luck, he decided to work on the material in his briefcase and mow the yard on Saturday.

As Sunday afternoon was about to give way to evening, he finished his paperwork and his domestic duties. Thinking of returning to his tree stand in the woods for a couple hours before dark, he decided against it. Feeling the unquestionable first hints of an approaching case of the flu, he would pass on the hunt. Tired, feeling ill and dejected, he realized that it would be his last opportunity to hunt for the Monarch of the Swamp. Perhaps in another three years he would again draw a license, and the Monarch would be a trophy.

As all serious hunters are prone to do, he succumbed to the urge. In haste, he decided to rush out to the stand for the remaining two hours of daylight, even though baiting would not be allowed. A creature of habit may return, especially in hopes of securing a few donuts. Parking his truck in the familiar spot, he grabbed his gear and advanced to the tree stand as fast as he could and climbed up the ladder.

Once there, he felt better. He breathed the autumn air deeply, relaxed and thought of his hard luck of the hunt. It had been a hunt to remember; the hours of baiting and trying to decipher a pattern for the bears, feeling the disappointment of being the only one of three hunters using the same guide to be unsuccessful. He had passed on a sure thing, had been interrupted on another, and had completely botched a third. He was due for some good luck.

As strange things happen while hunting in the woods, something caught his eye. A movement. A large figure moving slowly, and in his direction. Stepping out into the open 40 yards from his stand stood ... the game warden.

Boldly stepping forward, the warden inquired, "May I ask you what you are doing, sir?"

"Well, obviously I'm hunting," he answered trying not to sound insolent. "Bear hunting."

"I thought the season was closed," responded the warden, looking perplexed. Luckily he was not the warden who had cited a single mother for not having a fishing license as she cast her son's line for him to fish. And not the arrogant one who displayed his firearm prominently on his hip while resting his foot on the gunwale as he checked fishing licenses on Lake Superior. Shouting like a drill sergeant, he demanded those who were fishing to hold up their licenses for him to see.

"Well, the way I read the regs, you can't bait anymore, but you can still hunt through the weekend," responded the hunter.

"Come to think of it, I believe you're right. Those regs are really complicated this year," commented the warden. "And you're not using any bait now?"

"No sir!"

"Well then, what's this?" asked the warden as he pointed at a lone glazed donut hanging from the broken limb at the base of the tree.

"Oh shoot! I put it there on Friday when it was legal to bait, and I guess the bears missed it."

The warden smiled an understanding smile. "Doesn't matter

when you put it there, it's still bait," said the friendly warden as he reached for his citation book.

Since that day, he hasn't applied for another bear license nor had a craving for bear-claw donuts.

The Heat is On

"Amateurs!" scoffed the old conservation officer good-naturedly. They were having coffee one morning at the Fearless Leader's restaurant last summer and were engaged in a congenial discussion on one of their favorite subjects, game warden games.

He was as fond of telling the tales as the Fearless Leader was listening to them. "Well, not long ago we had a stake-out goin' with the remote-controlled deer. And don't you know that along comes a hunter who happened to look at lot like the owner of this fabled eating establishment."

"I'll be darned!" responded our Fearless Leader with a slight blush.

"When you and that new guy stopped to look over the decoy, I thought I finally was goin' to catch you doin' somethin'. Well, after you leave, we don't nab anybody taking a shot at the decoy, and we couldn't figure out why. Well, shoot, as we're leavin' we see that some joker had made hand-written cardboard signs, or I should say hand-scribbled signs that say 'deer decoy ahead.' Can you imagine that?"

"You've got to be kidding!" chuckled the Mischievous One

while trying to give his best impression of someone being both surprised and disgusted. "Who would do a dastardly thing like that? It wasn't me 'cause I can write a whole lot better than that," he said with a sly smile while his dimples deepened. "Got any other good ones?" he asked sheepishly.

"Oh, heck yeah! This one is even better," continued the big guy as he added sugar to his coffee. "Couple years back I got this videotape in the mail so I stuck it in the VCR, and I about dropped my drawers. It's a video showin' this farmhouse with a bunch of wild turkeys in the yard. They were really pretty tame, you see. Then a couple of your huntin' buddies stick their shotguns out of the pickup window and start blastin' away at the turkeys. So then I see your buddy jump out of a truck and he grabs a couple birds by the neck. They're still flappin' around like crazy and he's a cacklin' like you wouldn't believe. I'd recognize that laugh anywhere. In the truck he jumps, and it takes off throwing gravel all over and the dust is just a flyin'.

Meanwhile, you see this old farmer come out of the farmhouse with his double-barreled shotgun, and he starts blazin' away at your truck as you're speedin' away. So, I'm shocked as all get out that you guys would do something as crazy as shootin' turkeys out of a farmer's front yard in broad daylight. And I'm amazed that it's caught on tape. I kinda suspected you guys for a long time, but I could never catch you doing anything wrong. Anyway, I start thinkin' about how many things I could cite you for, but then I got a little suspicious since the tape was sent without a return address. And my address is written by someone with poor penmanship that looked really familiar."

"To make a long story short, I found out that you guys had actually paid the farmer generously for the turkeys. He helped you stage and tape the whole darned thing and then someone – I never found out who – sends me the tape thinkin' I'd believe it was the real thing, I guess."

Laughing as he pushed his hat back on his head, he rubbed

his chin. "That video deal was a fairly good one," he added. His Howdy Doody-ish face was tanned and wind burned since he spent so much time in the field. We all knew that, like a lot of other DNR folks, he actually spent lots of additional unpaid and unrecognized hours performing the job he loved.

"I gotta admit that one wasn't bad, but you local guys are still amateurs when it comes to witty stunts," he said. "You'll never come close to matching the kinds of things wardens pull on each other. Let me give you an example," he said as he related the story:

"So we're having a real live dog and pony show today at the Post meeting, isn't that just peachy keen?" complained Ed, a senior CO.

"Afraid so," responded his lieutenant, who runs the monthly meetings. "And guess what? We have to keep the darned dog in the building all day according to the little dolly who trained him. When I was growing up, dogs lived outdoors. I'm sure as heck glad nobody's bringing a pony!"

As in many long-standing organizations, the established leadership at this regional DNR office was definitely "old school." Having worked his way up through the ranks over the years, Ed was an old military leader in a non-military situation, and he also kept physically fit. He had learned both in the Marine Corps. Being a "body count" kind of guy, he had decided long ago not to take any guff from anyone, not even the political appointees who headed the DNR. It's interesting to note that he got along well with the lieutenant to whom he reported. They had a lot in common. Ed was a legend, and any changes under his command would progress about as quickly as the flow of cold molasses.

A dynamic and articulate dog handler who was proud of her position and eager to demonstrate the value of the new K-9 program was scheduled to speak at the monthly meeting. Realizing that funding for the new endeavor came from the budgets of traditional programs, she was aware of scattered resentment toward her "doggie" program among the old boys. But she had grown up with three older brothers and could take care of herself extremely well.

"Lieutenant, I'm here to do our K-9 demonstration, and this is 'Heat,' my companion," she said as she entered his small office.

"That so? Is the cutesy name lamely designed to intimidate game offenders, or is it the state of your doggie's biological cycle?" asked the lieutenant with gross sarcasm. Ed chuckled.

"Well, my dog is a male, so that rules that out doesn't it?" bristled the handler looking him squarely in the eyes. She regretted having fallen into the trap.

"Well, you just can't let your doggie roam around the office all day. I've got a meeting to run, so find a place to secure him and have a seat in the conference room. I'll call on you when it's time for you to do your thing."

Hooking the young German shepherd's leash on the doorknob of the conference room's back door, she took a chair next to a young man whom she had met at the department's headquarters. She knew that he was one of the bright young career professionals, well educated and progressive in his thinking. He was also a quiet type who impressed her with his courtesy and impeccable uniform, which he wore proudly. He represented the new breed of conservation officers in every way.

"I see you're on the hot seat today," said Ron as they exchanged pleasantries.

"Yeah, I kinda feel like I'm going into the lion's den with my K-9 demonstration. No doubt that most of the COs will welcome the program. It's just those two in charge who bother me."

"Those guys aren't all that bad, just a couple of old schoolers. It's going to take a while. But they'll come around, you just wait and see."

"Yeah, I suppose you're right," she responded, though less than fully convinced.

"But," he cautioned, "you've got to challenge them whenever you see an opportunity. Remember that. Some of these old guys have done it the hard way and they're resistant to change. However, you'll find that their hearts are in their work, and they're a good bunch of guys who will back you all the way once you get through the barriers."

"I suppose you're right, but it's hard not to be irritated at their insensitivity," she replied as she turned around to check on Heat.

Meanwhile, the small conference area was filling, and Ed stood in the doorway at the rear of the room to take a census of the attendees. He frowned at Heat as the well-groomed dog walked closer and stood next to him as if he had in mind substituting Ed's leg for a fire hydrant.

Pouring a last-minute cup of coffee before the meeting was to begin; Ron noticed the dog's position and chuckled to himself. While being mild-mannered and professional, he couldn't resist the temptation. Strolling into the side kitchen area he soon exited behind the door where Ed stood with Heat positioned strategically next to his leg.

He dribbled the warm water obtained from the kitchen onto the leg of Ed's trousers. The spots immediately turned dark in color. Stepping back, Ron loudly exclaimed, "Oh, Ed! Look what that darned dog has gone and done."

"What the … Damnation! Look what that mutt did to my uniform. Lieutenant, will you look at this? For crying out loud! That dog done peed all over my leg."

Laughter filled the room as everyone turned to see Ed's wet pant leg. Turning around and spying the unbelievable sight, Heat's handler gasped. The commotion infuriated the impatient lieutenant whose meeting was set to begin.

"Handler, get that dog out of here," shouted the veteran bureaucrat.

Annoyed at the dog's apparent action, she responded, "Sorry

lieutenant, I can't believe it! I know he's trained better than that. I don't know what got into him."

"Just get that stupid dog out of here right now!" bellowed the lieutenant, exercising his authority.

Gazing at the human interactions and wearing a somewhat quizzical look, Heat suddenly took the heat by having his neck stretched about two inches as the handler jerked on his leash and headed toward the door. Heat yelped as he was quickly hauled outside amid further delighted laughter.

Meanwhile, the impish instigator was about to explode at the comedy. It was perfect! But he hadn't intended to see the highly skilled dog exiled to the cold truck for the duration of the meeting, and he also felt guilty about getting the handler in trouble with the lieutenant. So out the door he went to confess that Heat had not been the perpetrator of the episode.

"You did that? You don't seem like the kind of guy who would pull a stunt like that," said the weary handler. "You sure put me in a bad spot with the lieutenant. Thanks a lot! I'm feeling really embarrassed at having been chastised in front of everyone. And think of poor Heat. Everyone was laughing at him, and I handled him pretty rough. I think you should at least tell the lieutenant what really happened in there."

"I suppose that's fair on my part. I've got to say it sure was funny, though, seeing old Ed carrying on and dancing around with his pant leg all wet. I hope the lieutenant doesn't tell him the whole story."

Ron explained to the lieutenant what had really happened. He was surprised that Ron was the instigator of such a disruptive production.

"I've got to say it was pretty clever all right. The look on Ed's face was hilarious! Everybody needs a little humor now and then, but I'll thank you in advance for not disrupting any more of my meetings."

"Sorry lieutenant, I just couldn't pass up the opportunity

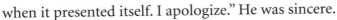
when it presented itself. I apologize." He was sincere.

Having talked to the handler and the lieutenant, Ron felt better since he had smoothed over relations with half of the innocent bystanders involved in the incident.

Chuckling to himself as he recalled the event and Ed's reaction to it, he was waiting for the month's meeting to begin. The young CO had gotten plenty of comments about the wet-leg comedy but had not had to face Ed. He hoped the lieutenant hadn't spilled the beans.

Suddenly, there was a sharp and deliberate tapping on his shoulder, and he turned around and gazed up into the *Semper Fi* eyes of none other than Ed.

"Well, young feller, you'll be interested to know that I'm coming around to some of these new enforcement ideas. Sometimes it takes us old guys a while. You'll be pleased to hear that I even had me a long, long talk with that darned dog, and do you know what? He and I discovered that we have something in common. Me and that ol' doggie agree," he said as he smiled and leaned closer to Ron and with determination exclaimed, "we both agree that payback is gonna be hell!"

Life After Deer Season

The deer gods must have been smiling on him once again during deer season. A combination of outdoor skills and a little luck helped Moose Rider win the local big buck contest sponsored by the Fearless Leader's "tav-ern." But the new warden was coming to town at the first of the year, and his good luck was about to run out.

Groans and gurgles were being emitted from the scenic lake after an overnight temperature of minus thirteen. The eerie sounds signaled ice making and the approaching conclusion of the calendar year. It was the time of year to stow away deer rifles and tree stands. Life was returning to normal. Serenity was overtaking the North Country and preserving it in frigid temperatures, like newly processed venison sausage stored in the freezer.

In the early morning darkness, sounds carried across our frozen lake with the sharpness of a fillet knife. Gas-powered ice augers were already at work down the lake. Their whine reached Moose Rider long after he began fishing. He arrived earlier than usual to place his tip-ups in a long row that stretched out into the darkness. Had he heard that the walleyes were biting early? Likely he would not have advertised it if he had heard such a

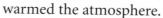

rumor, but certainly he would have checked it out. Why else would he be on the ice that early?

Wood smoke from the cozy cabins dotting the western shore drifted over the lake, and the sweet smell of burning birch logs was in the air. Fires in icehouse stoves also produced gray plumes of wood smoke that rolled lazily out of crude metal chimneys and added to a layer of haze. It would soon dissipate as the sun warmed the atmosphere.

Activity was increasing. Red and blue plastic sleds were being dragged across the ice by bundled figures in groups of two or more. Others drove four-wheelers onto the ice, and still others were trudging through the snow with huge packs on their backs looking like Russian soldiers marching off to the revolution in a Tolstoy novel. A raven flew over the highway on its morning patrol for roadkill.

During the preceding evening at the "tav-ern," the game warden had stopped to pick up a pizza. It was one of their specialties, and he purchased a large pepperoni on his way home every Friday night. Spotting Moose Rider, and having maintained a mutual and respectable relationship with him for over 20 years, the warden wandered around the wooden bar to his stool. It was directly below the gaze of the mounted bobcat which the Gentle Warrior had taken several years ago.

"Heard you got the winning buck again this year," offered the warden as his greeting. Standing about six-feet-six, he is an imposing figure in uniform. Intimidating to some. "I suppose it was a legal buck you shot and not one you had penned up somewhere?"

"Yep! Pull up a stool and open up that pizza, and I'll tell you all about it," quipped Moose Rider. "But it's gonna be a long story."

Moose Rider had always been an extremely successful outdoorsman and often been suspected of, shall we say, stretching the game limits. However, he had never been cited for anything illegal. Rather enjoying the reputation, he fed fuel to the fire at times just to make life more interesting, one would presume. Practical jokes and horseplay were not foreign to Moose Rider. He thrived on them. But who worked harder on local conservation activities or putting out a local brush fire than Moose Rider? Who else would be more inclined to play a trick on the warden than Moose Rider?

There is something to be said about the relationship between a sportsman and a warden who have known each other for years and who enjoy sparring with each other. It's like the wolf and deer, a predator and prey relationship. However, with Moose Rider and the warden, it was often hard to tell which one was the hunter or the hunted.

During his arduous career, the warden had been shot at three times, and he figured that was enough. Upon retiring, he planned on traveling to warmer climates. Later he might go into teaching; or perhaps he'd write a book on the escapades he had experienced during his years in the field. He hadn't decided.

Meanwhile, clutching the warm cardboard pizza box, the warden said, "Well, I'd like to sit and visit but I gotta get this pizza back to the house before the bride sends out a search party." He was not about to fall for the bait. "You'll have to come to my retirement party in two weeks and three days. But who's counting? There'll be lots of pizza there and maybe even a brewski or two."

"I heard you had to resort to bribing people with food and beer in order to get anyone to show up," chuckled Moose Rider.

Sitting around the bar, locals looked up from their glasses of beer and smiled.

"That's about it," grinned the warden. "By the way, if you're gonna be on the lake tomorrow, I'll be showing my replacement around. I want to make sure he gets to know the local area, and I especially want him to have a chance to meet you," he added with a laugh. "You're already on his most-wanted list, and he hasn't even met you yet."

"I'll be there. Bring him by for lunch. I'd love to have him," responded Moose Rider. That brought a round of hearty laughter from the plaid-shirted customers seated nearby. They were familiar with the game. They loved it.

Long ago, when the warden had first moved to town, he felt resentment and anger when one of the legendary locals lured him into a prank. Later, he mellowed and actually enjoyed the challenge. It gave him plenty of stories to tell when he gathered with his associates. Many times he had the best story to share. He wished he had kept notes on all the North Country shenanigans. They would have made writing a two-volume book easy.

That's the way it had been for the past 20+ years. Now the proverbial "new guy" would take over and each antagonist would have to develop the relationship from square one, like two young bucks establishing a home range in adjacent forties. The relationship would involve give and take. It would mature over time.

At eight o'clock the next morning, the familiar olive-green sport utility vehicle bearing the fish and game insignia crawled onto the ice and hesitated. Warm exhaust gasses billowed around the rear of the SUV. Peering through his binoculars, the passenger in the front seat scanned the lake from end to end. Aligning the truck's tires with the ruts in the snow and ice, the warden swung the vehicle to the south and headed for the nearest ice hole. After a brief stop and a quick license check, he turned the vehicle toward the faded red ice shack belonging to the legendary Moose Rider.

Small banks of ice and snow crunched under the vehicle's weight as it crossed the frozen lake. As it came to a slow stop, the snow squeaked under the tires like a hundred possessed mice. Both occupants climbed out and greeted their host.

The new warden was not a rookie just out of school. Rumor had it that he had come from the county just to the south of Madison. Would he play the game strictly by the rules?

Cleanly shaven and direct in his manner, he could have been in the Marine Corps, or perhaps a Green Beret in his early years. His large frame was erect, and he wore stylish but masculine sunglasses. Speaking in a manner as crisp as the morning air, his eyes scanned the lake as he spoke. He didn't miss any details.

Exchanging weather talk, the three figures conversed while the truck continued to idle. Shortly, the retiring warden said that he was going to see what was happening at the north end of the lake and to check licenses.

"I'll be back in 15 or 20 minutes," he advised while climbing into the truck and engaging the transmission. "Man, I'm sure not going to miss these cold days. My arthritis has been giving me fits for years. Next year when you guys are on the ice freezing your butts, I'm gonna be lying on a warm beach somewhere." Grinning, he said, "You guys behave while I'm gone."

"I'll keep an eye on him for you," joked Moose Rider as he emptied his coffee cup. Brown stains appeared where the warm coffee met the ice. "Want some coffee, partner?" he asked the new guy whose eyes were following the movement of the truck down the lake. The warden seemed uncomfortable.

"No, thanks, sir."

"How about a little shot of 'snaps'?" asked the Moose Rider, pulling a new pint of peppermint schnapps from a pocket inside his fringed buckskin jacket.

Scrutinizing him in disbelief, the new warden declined in a polite but professional manner. "No, thank you, sir, not while I'm on the job."

"Wanna bucket to sit on?" offered the fisherman as he pointed to a five-gallon bucket containing a solitary tip-up. He lowered himself into an ancient and somewhat crooked aluminum lawn chair.

"No, sir. He'll be back soon, but thanks anyway," replied the warden as he inspected Moose Rider's tip-up. His eyes then focused intently on the nearest tip-up that was rigged above a perfectly round hole created by Moose Rider's ice auger. He gazed back at Moose Rider sitting in his chair and pouring "snaps" into his coffee mug bearing the "tav-ern's" logo. Returning his attention to the tip-ups that were stretched out in a straight line to the west, the warden's head bobbed up and down slowly as he counted each one. Counting them again slowly and deliberately he repeated the head nods.

"Anybody fishing with you today, sir?" asked the warden nonchalantly.

"Yep! My brother Bebe and Zinn, the Zinger." The latter had earned his name after harvesting his first deer – still bearing spots – the previous season. "They should be here any minute, as a matter of fact."

"Well, if I counted correctly, you have nine tip-ups out there."

"Yep! That's right, three per angler," agreed Moose Rider. "That's what the regulations say is legal."

"Yes sir, but nobody else is here, and you have more lines set than you are allowed," said the warden. "It appears to me that you are in violation of the code, sir," he continued while looking toward Moose Rider for an exclamation.

Rising from his chair, the buckskin fisherman gazed down the row of tip-ups. "Geez! I thought for sure I set the legal number out. Anyway, the others will be here any minute."

"You can't do it that way, sir!" exclaimed the astonished warden. "I'm going to have to issue you a citation, sir. Please wait here while I collect your tip-ups for evidence."

"A man's gotta do what a man's gotta do," said Moose Rider as he sat back down in his rickety chair almost knocking over his schnapps. "Don't seem right to cite a man who ain't done nothin' wrong."

Walking in a brisk manner to the first tip-up, the DNR agent lifted it from the hole. A thin layer of ice shattered as he raised the device and started winding the braided nylon line onto the small reel on the end of the tip-up. When he finished, he removed the minnow and dropped it onto the ice. Flopping and wiggling frantically, the minnow made no progress in its attempt to escape. Laying the tip-up carefully down by the hole, the Warden moved on to the second one. The process was repeated again and again in the same manner.

Old Moe, one of the elder statesmen of the Fearless Leader's hunting party, observed the proceedings from his shanty and came outside with his binoculars to investigate further. Curiosity was one of his strong assets.

At the fourth hole, the warden reeled up the line, but as he completed the task, he discovered that it was missing a hook. Tucking the orange flag of the tip-up in its place, he laid the instrument next to the hole. Off he went to hole number five.

As he reached the next location, he lifted the tip-up and repeated the process of carefully winding the line as it emerged from the dark depths. His fingers were bare and must have been getting cold. Lifting the end of the hook-less fishing line he examined it carefully as if to discover why there was nothing attached to its end. Directing a look at Moose Rider, he saw that he was still seated in his leaning lawn chair. According to the other fishermen who were emerging from their houses and watching silently, neither man blinked. Turning toward the next hole, he strode with determination.

Reaching the sixth hole, the warden did not wind the line on the reel but lifted the tip-up and brought the line in hand-over-hand. No hook! He dropped the tip-up and eyed the fisherman who was on his feet watching the warden with the intensity of a wolf studying an injured deer. Turning toward the remaining tip-ups, the warden hesitated. Slowly at first, then increasing his stride, he approached the seventh hole, and again the line came up hand-over-hand only to reveal an absence of terminal tackle.

There are some who claim that the warden swore; others theorize that he was getting cold and already tired of winter, as he muttered something about "sunny beaches of Damascus." Once again, he glanced back at Moose Rider as if to get a signal of some kind. The angler stared back without emotion as if he were playing poker.

Returning from the highway, the raven landed high in a black spruce tree. Like a sinister judge dressed in black, he looked down at the proceedings and cocked his head sideways as if presiding. Croaking three times, he appeared to be watching the warden. The tense scene would have brought a smile to Poe's face.

Well, the warden was faced with two more tip-ups, having found only three baited hooks on the seven lines that he had checked. He halted, pulled his mittens from his parka and inserted his hands. He seemed to be buying time like an astute public speaker trying to think of a response to a tough question before answering. Aware that several fishermen were watching him, he moved on. Approaching the eighth hole, he lifted the tip-up tentatively and began winding the reel. Reaching the end of the line, he simply dropped the tip-up and appeared to issue a deep sigh. Perhaps it was a sigh of resignation. Perhaps a sigh of anger. One could not be sure since, by that time, he had walked more than 200 yards away from where he had started the tip-up trap line. His head began bobbing up and down as if he were barking commands to new recruits undergoing basic training. Old Moe could not be sure of the words the warden used, but it is doubtful that they could have been printed if he had.

Facing the last tip-up, he marched onward with resolution. Holding back at the final hole, he turned his head briefly toward Moose Rider who lifted his schnapps-filled mug high in the air as if he were proposing a toast. Lowering his head slightly, the warden looked around in all directions as if to determine how many fishermen were watching. Perhaps he hoped there were none. Once more he bent over. Up came the last line, hand-over-hand.

With the aid of binoculars steadied on the side of his fish-house, Old Moe reported that a smile appeared on the warden's face. Then his arms dropped to his side, his shoulders sagged and he threw the tip-up on the ice.

The raven uttered two judicial croaks, then flew away to resume his gruesome vigil over the empty highway.

Moose Rider was legal! Turning around, the warden began his slow, embarrassing march back to the ice shack. He had been beaten, and to make matters worse, his partner had returned to the shanty and was climbing out of the state-owned vehicle. Moose Rider wore the proverbial smile of a Chessie cat.

Kicking at random clumps of snow as he continued, the new warden moved under the gaze of at least a dozen fishermen who were attracted by the event and the return of the warden's vehicle. He managed a smile, but it was a smile of bitterness and embarrassment. A smile of defeat. He had met Moose Rider and Moose Rider had prevailed.

"What's he doing out there?" inquired the old warden as they stood watching the dejected new guy approach. "Did I miss something?"

"You missed it all right! I was keeping those extra tip-ups in the water to prevent them from freezing up until Bebe and Zinn, the Zinger, got here to fish for walleyes. But in the meantime, I caught me a sucker," replied the mischievous Moose Rider. That brought a puzzled look upon the face of his long-time friend.

"But you know what?" continued the Moose Rider as he pushed his hat back on his head, revealing his salt and pepper hair, "I kinda like this new fella! I think we're gonna get to know each other really well."

Part VIII: End of the Deer Trail

Caught in the Act

I was afraid that I would get caught in the act some day. And I did.

It was early afternoon in the North Country, and the sun shone brilliantly in the cobalt sky. Promising hints of spring were in the cool air, and the long winter's accumulation of snow eroded and dripped off of the garage roof. Cold droplets created a cacophony of sound on the roof of the hibernating hunting truck that was still surrounded by a foot of the white stuff. The drops continued on their path to the ground and carved a small ravine through the packed snow and ice on the sidewalk leading to the storage shed. On the other side of the walk, the snowmelt disappeared under a deep drift.

That's where I spent some idle time on rare occasions, and I treasured the brief rendezvous with her. I went there during those special times when I had that feeling, that yearning to escape the present and to relive those old memories. I could trust her to lift my spirits. I've had so many good times with her that it was no wonder that such a strong bond had been formed.

The classy lady had been around the proverbial block a few times to be sure and had the wrinkles to prove it. Let's just say that she was "mature." She had gotten me out of a few tight spots in the past, but she could not help with the issue at hand, which was trying to clarify why I was sitting there with her on that sunny afternoon. There was no doubt in my mind that my wife wouldn't understand if I tried to explain.

You see, the wife spied us while she was walking across the driveway to take out the trash. After a few paces, she did a double take as if she could not believe her eyes. We were busted!

Everyone knows that guys aren't worth a hoot at explaining our feelings; it's as unnatural as stopping to ask for directions. So just how does a guy try to rationalize that special secret relationship between a hunter and that other special gal in his life – his trusty deer hunting truck?

Although deer season was long past, I went out to spend a few minutes to reminisce. Her steering wheel has been worn smooth, and her windshield has several hard-luck chips. My eyes roamed over her features. Fly-removing forceps hung from the radio knob, a white rubber skirt from a bass spinnerbait had slowly melted on the dash that was littered with miscellaneous hunting and fishing gear. A decoy anchor and its cord occupied the ashtray, and sand from the late fall duck hunts covered her mismatched floor mats. One of the original mats had been discarded when the Fearless Leader opened a new bottle of fox urine cover scent. One whiff and he jerked it away so fast that he spilled some on the passenger-side floor mat. It had to go. Sunlight has robbed her seat covers of most of their original color, and their corners have become frayed. To me she is a thing of pure beauty.

Her glove box – one of the mammoth ones they used to make – is stuffed full of hunting regulations, coffee-stained topo maps, and God knows what else. I have no desire to clean it out.

Empty aluminum cans underneath her seat rattled in unison whenever we crossed railroad tracks or bounced along North Country back roads in search of whitetails. They were likely stored there after celebrating a prized brookie caught during a late afternoon sojourn to the Brule River. Without doubt, the cans share the space with spent rifle cartridges, bottles of mosquito and tick repellant, empty shotgun shells and a few token candy bar wrappers. I like it that way; it's as comforting to me as my living room recliner.

We've shared many nights camped under the wondrous Northern Lights, the mystical, magical *aurora borealis*. Wanting to better understand them, I had researched the phenomenon but found that the scientific explanation was irrelevant to the wonder and awe experienced when the skies are ablaze during the North Country deer season.

We've made excursions up Minnesota's North Shore for smelting and shore casting for lakers, as well as sojourns up the Gunflint Trail toward Ely, the gateway to the Boundary Waters Canoe Area. There were frequent expeditions to Michigan's Pere Marquette and Little Manistee in pursuit of steelhead and salmon. Road trips were made to South Dakota for pheasant opener and to the nameless potholes of North Dakota in search of honkers and snow geese. Future trips? Of course! Can't wait to give Saskatchewan's monster whitetails a try. But not all trips were as exotic as these.

Getting stuck while searching for blueberries, wild mushrooms and potholes filled with bluebills, was always a memorable event. Hundreds of scratches have marred her surface while scouting for new deer hunting sites. How about the time spent just kicking back and relaxing at the wheel and singing along off key with the radio? Think about the photographs of those big white-tailed bucks lying in her bed and the memories associated with special hunts? How can one explain the gratification of all those adventures?

On the other hand, why bother trying to explain? When cabin fever strikes, get out there and sit for a while and experience the hunt, relive the memories. Feel her and inhale her odor and think of all the great times you've spent together in the field. It may sound corny and more than a little weird, but try it some-time. Positive results are guaranteed!

Let me caution you, though. Try to do it in a place and at a time when you won't get caught. Otherwise, you'll have a hard time trying to explain what you're doing. Trust me!

Moose Hunt

Hunting for the largest member of the deer family – the unpredictable and sometimes cantankerous moose – would be one of my most memorable experiences. Likely for me as well as the poor moose!

While I was shooting lots of photos of his semi-tame wild turkey, my neighbor and I became friends, and he was kind enough to call me anytime a photo opportunity developed. Last winter something was tearing up the fences around his private wildlife management area, and he suspected a moose but doubted that one could live there without being spotted. Too many people lived nearby. But on a misty February morning when he was touring his sanctuary, a young bull moose charged out of the thicket. What a surprise!

Hoping to get some compensation for the damage to his fences, he called the DNR to explain the situation. He didn't want the magnificent creature to be hurt, but he also was incurring a lot of damage to his property and wondered if they could help. Their bureaucratic reply was, he said with a grin, "All you can do is enjoy him."

"You gotta come over and see this," said my friend on the

phone. "He's living by the pond right in the middle of the section and nobody knows he's there." Although houses lined all four borders of the square-mile section, the young bull had taken up residence in the thick willows and alders in the center, which was swampy and included a five-acre pond. "You should be able to get some good pictures of this dude. He's huge!"

Hunting a big moose with a camera seemed like the perfect thing to do on a winter weekend, so I accepted his invitation and showed up early on Saturday to set up a blind from which to shoot. Spending several unproductive hours cramped inside the portable blind while the moose stayed deep in cover gave me the incentive to think of a better approach to getting some photos. I came to the conclusion that if the moose was going to stay in the thick vegetation, I'd have to go in after him. Which I did.

Approaching the thicket with some trepidation, I had the camera loaded and was ready to shoot. It seemed pretty easy. After all, how well could a large gangly animal like a moose conceal himself in the spindly trees? The answer is, quite well. I didn't even see him until he bolted. Head held high, he seemed to have an indignant look in his eyes as he headed south. Not missing a stride, he didn't even slow his pace as he stepped over the damaged barbed wire fence. Engaging the motor drive, I lit up the Kodachrome and captured a dozen photos that later revealed images that may have passed for modern art. They weren't the high-quality, cover-page photos I had hoped for. I'd have to try an even riskier approach to get closer to him.

I previously had a few close encounters with moose. Once when a buddy and I were in the Boundary Waters Canoe Area, a young bull spotted us as we fished for walleyes in the narrows between two lakes. Staring at us from a growth of conifers a hundred yards away, he slowly approached until he was a mere 30 yards from us at the water's edge. There was no reason to believe he would come out into the water toward us, but that is exactly what he did after pausing at the water's edge and staring at us for a couple of minutes. When he splashed headlong into the current, we hoisted the anchor while shouting like banshees. Fortunately, he halted in knee-deep water and stared as we got the heck out of there. And on another occasion while traveling a remote road in northern Minnesota at dusk, a huge bull ran directly in front of my red T-Bird, but I locked the brakes up in time to prevent a real mess for both of us. A bull moose can tip the scales at 1200 pounds, and collisions with vehicles are pretty ugly.

After much contemplation, I decided that if my moose left the security of his hiding place he wouldn't venture out in the open for too long during broad daylight without wanting to return to his hideout. So all I had to do to get some shots was to wait for him to reappear once he spooked. That was just what I did.

Clear skies and cold temperatures greeted the February morning, and I was ready for action. Marching directly in the thickest stands of young aspen and birch – favorite fare of the moose – I listened and watched with anticipation. It wasn't long before the awkward giant burst out of the cover and headed around the far side of the frozen pond. Nostrils flaring and steaming, his beady little eyes glared at me as he lumbered by. How awesome and intimidating to have to look up into the eyes of the animal one is hunting. And I planned to wait for the huge beast to return to take his picture!

Searching for the most photographically pleasing spot to shoot the disturbed moose upon his return, I found a site next to the ice-covered pond. A finger of ground projected into the pond to create a small bay between me and the trail that the moose would hopefully take on his return. In essence, the ice-covered bay created a safety barrier between us. But in order to get to my chosen site, I had to pass through a small stand of ash trees. Fortunately, it contained one tree big enough to climb. In addition, I would have to go through a fence. The top strand of barbed wire remained, although the middle and bottom strands had both been damaged when the moose apparently stepped on them. But if he came back the way he departed, I'd have a great opportunity for photos as well as a good escape route.

The frozen edge of the pond provided a pleasing backdrop of dormant reeds and cattails, which were abundant on the far side of my protective bay. The trail passing near the pond's edge allowed a full-frame shot of the moose from the knees up. If he stayed on the trail.

Pouring my morning coffee from my stainless steel thermos, I checked the camera for proper exposure and reviewed my escape route. I'd have to sprint through the thick brush, dive through the fence, rush beyond the trees, turn to the right and climb the biggest ash tree ... pronto. Judging the distance from the moose's trail, I figured there would be enough time to escape should his poor eyesight or unpredictability lead to a confrontation. I had the feeling that one was about to occur.

Sitting on my stool on that frosty morning and searching the dense vegetation across the bay, I thought how amazing it is that a large animal can hide and suddenly appear in the wild and how quietly one can travel. Sure enough, the first thing that caught my eye was the movement of his brownish antlers. I hadn't heard a sound. He was cautiously making his way back to safety. As he eased into the opening across the little bay, the moose offered a full-frame shot. That was the moment I had been anticipating. I tried to control my shaking hands, hold my breath and engage the motor drive. Zap! Zap! Zap!

Spooked by the sound of the advancing film, the moose became skittish and retreated with his head lowered. Another 10 minutes passed and the scene was repeated. I was getting some tremendous shots, and he was less nervous than before. Less nervous perhaps than me, but again he lowered his big head and retreated.

Although moose are said to have poor eyesight, he could

definitely see me – no doubt about it. And, he could see that I was too close for him to feel secure enough to sneak back to his safe hiding spot. But I stood my ground, and the next time he appeared, he decided to stand his ground. There we were.

I reviewed my escape plan for the sixth time. He was gigantic even though only a youngster. Turning his head away to look toward his rear and then back again at me it was as if he was reviewing his own escape route. After another round of head turns and full-frame shots he faced me, and moved toward the pond's edge just inches from the ice. One more step and he would be there, and I'd be gone. Peering through the narrow field of vision of the telephoto lens, and periodically changing film, meant that I couldn't keep my eyes on him all the time. However, I concluded that if he charged at me he would have to cross the bay, so my alert signal would be the sound of breaking ice. As I refocused the telephoto lens the ice shattered, and my heart leaped. Yikes!

Grabbing the tripod and holding my breath, I tried to propel my Arctic-pak boots through the snow and thick vegetation. Try that sometime! I dove for the fence. Feeling the dizzy rush of whatever levels of adrenaline the body releases when a moose is after you I passed under the fence, but my progress and escape came to an abrupt halt. The hood of my down parka had become impaled on the top strand of barbed wire, and I was bent over, arms full of equipment and stuck. Instantly the sickening feeling of panic engulfed me. Tugging didn't help, and the hopelessness of trying to slip out of my parka flashed through my mind. Time wouldn't permit it. But an extra dose of adrenaline shot through my body, and I lunged ahead hearing a snapping sound as the hood separated from the parka. Out of breath and panicked, I cleared the fence, passed through the stand of ash, and made the right-hand turn to my climbing tree.

At that point, I reluctantly dropped the equipment and glanced back to assess whether I had time to get into the tree, just enough time to hide behind it, or neither. My hood was gently waving in the breeze on the rusting strand of fence. Back at the pond's edge stood the moose. He hadn't moved a single step! Hadn't budged at all! Standing and staring at me from the other side of my escape bay, he held his head high. His eyes were not glaring, but he didn't take them off of me as I sat down on the frozen ground and laughed out loud. The bewildered moose must have watched the whole incident in amazement and thought to himself, "I wonder what the heck got into that crazy human! You just can't trust them! Yet they're the ones who say a moose's behavior is unpredictable!"

Smoke Pole Hunting

I can't tell you how many years I owned a muzzleloader before I finally took it into the field deer hunting. I simply don't remember. But how could I ever forget that first hunting adventure with the ol' smoke pole?

"I've got permission for a new huntin' spot," said my son-in-law. But there was a catch. "Hopefully, we can find it in the dark. Do you want to give the smoke poles a try early tomorrow?"

There is a certain romance about shooting with black powder. Although it doesn't make me feel much like a mountain man, frontiersman or voyageur, I do experience a certain closeness with my muzzle-loading rifle that I don't feel with my modern high-powered weapon. A muzzleloader, however, is not the kind of firearm that one gets thrilled about lugging around all day in the woods while deer hunting, especially in thick cover. It is a cumbersome, though handsome, firearm that forces one to concentrate on the ethical practice of making one shot count. That's all you get.

The late muzzleloader season had opened on a full moon amid mild temperatures. If global warming is a reality, late-season muzzleloaders will be high on the list of adamant supporters. It is far easier to hunt with a smoke pole on those rare occasions when you can feel each and every one of your fingers after hunting for a couple of hours during late December

During early autumn my son-in-law had taught me how to properly shoot and maintain my Hawkin .45 caliber, and I came to like the sulfurous smell of gunpowder. When I discharged the long rifle, I liked the thick cloud of smoke it spit out like a fire-breathing dragon. I was ready to deer hunt.

"I'll pick you up at 4:30 and that'll give us time to find the spot and get situated before sun-up," he said excitedly.

"Sounds good," I responded somewhat less excitedly, though willingly. "4:30 it is."

We were still getting to know each other and had only spent two days deer hunting during the regular firearms season. It had been cold and windy. That's all we can remember about those first hunts together. But with the muzzleloader deer season opening, we looked forward to hunting again, and the mild conditions would make charging and priming the oversized rifles a lot easier. It sounded like the perfect situation.

He arrived at the house right on time in the silent, pitch-black morning, and we debated about firing a couple of percussion caps in the guns to dry out any residual oil in the bores. Deciding to wait until we made the hour-long trip in the darkness toward our new hunting grounds, we left them in their cases and departed.

Pausing briefly at an all-night truck stop – where the pink-uniformed, divorced and tired waitresses call you "Hon" – we wolfed down an order of biscuits and gravy. Even a generous helping of hot sauce made it only semi-palatable, Hon! Future gastronomic reminders of breakfast were sure to follow. Burp!

Skillfully navigating directly to our newly acquired hunting spot, my son-in-law pulled his Chevy pickup through an open gate and doused the headlights. I burped. Unloading our gear in the darkness, we lamented the lost opportunity to fire a couple a caps at the truck stop or even at the poison-gravy waitress. He placed a percussion cap over the rifle's round nipple and detonated it with a sound approaching that of a small stick of dynamite disrupting the tranquil countryside. He squeezed off another, and I followed with one discharge and decided that it was enough. There probably weren't any deer remaining within two miles anyway.

We walked cautiously up the gradual hill and out onto a hardwood ridge between two ravines, stopping halfway to catch our breath. Shortly afterward, I staked out a spot behind a thick staghorn sumac stand, pulled out my binoculars, and arranged my gear. He continued southward toward the point of the ridge.

As the morning sun illuminated the countryside, I adjusted my location to conceal my presence. However, I maintained an unobstructed shooting lane through the maple trees as I overlooked the peaceful ravine. Breathing the damp morning air and listening to the natural morning sounds was comforting. Burping frequently was not, Hon.

As the sun rose higher, my face warmed as I enjoyed the solitude even though I had no idea where I was. I knew he would work his way back to my spot before lunchtime since he had other plans for the afternoon. The ravine remained peaceful, shadowed and inviting.

Around 11 o'clock, I saw his blaze orange jacket moving slowly in my direction. Stalking silently and deliberately, he approached as if reluctant to call it a day. Suddenly freezing and mouthing the word "deer," he nodded his head slightly toward the upper end of the ravine then slowly raised his arm and pointed.

Feeding casually were three whitetails that would have reached my line of sight within another minute or two. Fortunately, they did not spook. He had a clear shot, so he lowered himself to one knee, took aim and fired. His dragon spoke. The deer scampered about excitedly for a few moments, unable to determine where the blast came from. They stood, stamped their feet, watched and listened. It is common behavior for whitetails when a sudden, loud noise occurs and they can't comprehend what's happening. The frightened but unharmed whitetails wandered even closer to our location.

It was my turn. Raising my ol' smoke pole, I fought the buck-fever-producing excitement and hurriedly placed the trigger in the full-cock position, then leveled the rifle at the nearest basket-buck. Pulling the trigger in a gradual motion to release the smoky dragon's fire, I heard a piercing and sickening "click." Misfire! Or more accurately, no fire!

At the resounding metallic noise, the confused deer scampered about randomly until a doe finally presented herself broadside at half the distance as before. She stared intently in our direction for signs of movement while trying to locate our position, or perhaps discovering the source of the horrible breath wafting up the ravine.

He mumbled something about the importance of snapping

caps before charging a muzzleloader and struggled to quietly reload. I fumbled through my 30-pocket hunting jacket desperately searching for another percussion cap while fighting the growing urge to bust out laughing at the amusing fiasco. Before either of us could reload, the trio of white-tailed deer had heard, seen or smelled enough of us to cause them to depart headlong for the next county.

I didn't get another chance at a buck with the ol' smoke pole that year. The laughable calamity that heartburn morning was the only opportunity we had until the following season. We laugh heartily about it now. Although we can't remember much about our first firearms hunt together, we vividly remember our first smoke pole adventure, and we reminisce about it every deer season. And he always reminds me philosophically, "You only get one shot with the ol' smoke pole, you know … and that's why they call it hunting instead of killing."

White-Throated Treasures

While jigging for finicky walleyes during late May in the remote Canadian wilderness, it was gratifying to feel the north-westerly winds diminish and the waves subside to a gentle, harmless lapping against the canoe's bow. We had escaped from civilization earlier in the day on a sturdy float plane – an ancient Beaver – flying out of Sioux Lookout, Ontario. It is an annual spring ritual that I look forward to sharing with my deer hunting companions.

We awaited the evening walleye bite as the distant buzz of congregating mosquitoes indicated that darkness would soon envelop the rugged land. It was that magical hour just before sunset when tranquility prevails. It would soon be dark.

From the protection of dense conifers came the hearty, cherished call that sent my thoughts reeling six months ahead to white-tailed deer hunting season. It was the treasured melody of the white-throated sparrow.

Now one might conclude that white-throats don't have a lot in common with deer hunting, but I happen to think they do. By some coincidence of nature, both have white throats. And the spunky sparrow – that is in reality a finch – often lines its nest with deer hair. Those are good enough connections for me.

Feeding primarily on weed seeds, dogwood and cedar berries, and oak and maple buds, the secretive white-throat is often heard noisily scratching in the litter layer near running water or a lakeshore. One is more likely to hear its peaceful song than to spot one of the handsome little birds at this time of year. Forget about trying to settle the debate about whether it sings "Sweet Canada" or "Ol' Sam Peabody." Just listen and enjoy. Frequently vocalizing all day long, they are an essential element of spring walleye fishing in the North Country.

To me, the white-throat's call means that I'll soon be treated to the haunting, mystifying yodel of loons as they cut loose just before dark. Their tremolo and wailing calls arouse as much emotion as a Fourth of July parade when old veterans in ill-fitting uniforms march with passion and patriotism in their eyes and perseverance in their hearts. That is why I think of deer hunting when the white-throat sings.

Soon after the first of the year when scouring a sunny hillside for antler sheds, I was moved by the mysterious cries of the piliated woodpecker. Busily excavating roosting and nesting cavities, their raucous calls and machine-gun-like drumming are often the avian highlight of a frigid day. They seem to be trying to awaken the quiet land for a new spring season like a diligent biological alarm clock. They are also among my favorites.

What evening in the summer could be complete without the soothing song of the awesome wood thrush? Preferring the protection of the damp deciduous forest, his peaceful song, ending with a bell-like tinkle gives me comfort and heightens my appreciation for classical music. Still, I doubt that even a genius like Mozart could capture the liquid gold of the wood thrush's refrain. It is truly spiritual.

While deer hunting, I always smear a glob of peanut butter for the chickadees on a tree near my stand. The hearty birds seem happy with the free lunch, and their renowned song assures me that spring will eventually arrive. I also find it comforting that the flitting chickadee may line its nest with deer hair like the white-throat. Maybe there is some rhyme and reason to connecting birds with deer season. Maybe they aren't just coincidences of nature. It is something to contemplate when passing the silent hours in a lonely deer stand while waiting to hear the cheerful chickadee's song that will propel my thoughts ahead to spring and the white-throats.

My hunting companions tell me they have similar connections with birds. They really do! Fussy jays will frequently alert an observant deer hunter to a wary buck's quiet approach. Springtime drumming of the "partridge" not only provides qualitative information on the dramatic rise and fall of their populations, it also gives fall bird hunters an idea of where to find the ruffed grouse when season opens. Sandhill cranes flying in formation and continuously croaking their primitive call creates a sound that rings of innocence and wildness. Still, none of these examples is as heart warming to me as the white-throat's welcome call in the far North during a spring walleye ritual.

Conversely, when I am in my deer stand on a clear, frosty November morning and "chicka-dee-dee-dee" rings out, it completes nature's cycle for me. My mind returns to the ritual of spring walleye fishing in the Canadian wilderness.

I know that when I hear the white-throats sing again, I will have recovered from cabin fever, and the winter's snow will be nearly gone. When white-throats sing, I will be savoring their delightful song in a pristine bay of a remote Canadian wilderness lake. Indeed, when I hear the white-throats sing I will be feasting on golden walleye fillets, fried potatoes with their skins on, and baked beans kicked-up with a generous shot of hot pepper sauce. And when the white-throats sing, I will undoubtedly be thinking about hunting that other favorite mystical white-throat … the white-tailed deer. It all makes sense.

Next Year, I'm Gonna ...

Enough of this nonsense! Next year's deer season is gonna be different because I'll be prepared. Just wait and see!

I'm gonna start preparing for the next deer season as soon as this year's poorly planned disaster is over. This is the last time you'll see me unprepared, I guarantee it. Starting right away, I'll map out all of the rut route trails and major rubs while the leaves are gone and I can see the landscape. Besides that, following each significant snowfall, I'll venture out in the woods and see where the deer tracks are leading. Good idea, eh?

Right after the first of the year I'll be out there on the south-facing slopes looking for antler sheds on those mild, sunny days when snow is melting and there is a promise of spring in the air. And I'm going to keep records on each set of antlers that I find next year. For sure!

Definitely, I'm gonna mark my calendar with the dates of the bow, firearm, and muzzleloader deer seasons. Plus dates like the end of May when the does give birth to fawns. In addition, I'll add the dates when the bucks should start sparring and when the rut commences, plus the date I'll head to deer camp. They'll all be there on one handy calendar so I can plan ahead next year.

Why, I'll even clean out the garage ahead of time so when I bring that hefty buck home after tracking him late into the night, he'll be hanging up in no time. Never again am I gonna clear out the garage at night to make room to hang my deer. That's a promise!

No more fishing trips to Canada in the spring without a hefty supply of venison jerky, either. I'll make room by cleaning out the freezer ahead of time and donating any extra venison to the needy. Furthermore, I'll talk to my buddies and sample their processed venison goods and decide which meat market is going to make my jerky and summer sausage. I'll be prepared next time around.

I'm done with that business of having just one deer stand, too. Getting out to visit the landowners will be high on my "to do" list. I'll even offer to help mend fences or gates in return for permission to hunt, and we'll share in the bounty next year. For sure, I'll have the landowner give me a written letter of permission so if some wise guy tries to run me off by saying it's his land, I'll be prepared. No more panic on opening day when some clown parks in my secret spot either. I'll scout out some alternative parking sites next season.

Once I get permission to hunt on some promising land, I'll get the area topographic maps and might go as far as to get soil maps; maybe vegetation maps, too. By golly! I wonder if aerial photos are available? I'll find out. Next year, those cagey old bucks aren't going to have a chance.

Scouting my hunting sites with good binoculars and a notebook, I'll record deer movements, including feeding habits and bedding areas. The temperature, relative humidity, wind direction and speed will be written down on every scouting trip. I'll even remember to record the moon phases next year. I know! I've said that before, but this time I really do mean it. Honest!

When I figure out the patterns of deer movement, I'll take some time and select the best locations for my stands. Clearing shooting lanes and marking distances will be a good summer activity. No more undershooting! No more guessing distances, not during next year's deer season.

I'll search for a site for the early part of the season when the deer are feeding on mast, like apples and acorns. Later on, the old swamp where the clever bucks head for safety as soon as the lead starts flying will have a strategic stand. It's gonna be awesome.

Yes, I'm doing my homework right this time. Wind roses from the weather service will show me the wind frequency distributions, and that will help me select the perfect site. No more getting busted by a monster buck catching my scent. No more sitting at home because the wind is from the wrong direction.

Indeed! Those books and magazines are coming off the shelves next year, too. Like everyone else, I have an advanced deer hunting book that's collecting dust, but next year it will be read. Might even check out a couple videos on deer hunting techniques from the sports shop during one of those stormy summer days. Think ahead!

Meeting with the area wildlife biologist will be high on my "to do" list. This time I'll do it before she gets busy in the fall. And I won't put off reading them until the night before opener when we have those long discussions at deer camp about whether the laws have changed or not. Checking with her will also be a good reminder to review my notes from hunter safety class as well. Can't be too careful out there. You know what I mean?

Who knows? I might find some time to devote to deer management or wildlife conservation projects or to help raise money by collecting deer hides. Next year I'll give something back. We all should give something back.

Shooting my bow will start early next spring. Probably even get me one of those life-size deer targets to increase my accuracy. If I have to take my bow to the shop for tuning next year, I'll do it early. I won't wait until a week before opening day again when the archery shop is overloaded. No problem!

Sighting in my gun isn't gonna be done at the last minute either. Summer will be filled with lots of practice. I'll try several different brands of ammo and see what works best for me. Meanwhile, I'll learn how to read ballistics graphs and understand them for once! I'll lay in a sufficient supply of ammunition so I won't have to run to the sporting goods store on the way to sight in my firearm. Next year, my friend, we will take no prisoners!

During those lush autumn days before season opener next fall, I'll be practicing grunting and rattling. I'll even get me one of those audiotapes to review so that I get it right. I'll play it in the truck when heading for the tree stand. And one lazy afternoon I'll just climb in the stand and practice turning my head real slow so I won't be detected by a big buck like I was two years ago. Busted big time!

Furthermore, marking and clearing my trail into my deer stands will keep me from crashing through the woods like a Yeti on opening morning. Next year I might even go out and just try walking through the woods as quietly as I can so I won't be spooking that monster buck again. Not during next year's deer season!

Washing my hunting clothes and storing them properly will be high on the list next year. No whiteners are going to touch those bad boys, not any more. Some of my excess blaze orange might actually go to Goodwill. If there is some new gear that I need, I'll look for the sales this fall after season closes. Don't need any sticker shock on the day before next year's opener. Might even drop some hints before my birthday or perhaps with Mrs. Claus just before Christmas. Heck of a good idea! Try it!

Can't forget to make a check-off list of gear to take to deer camp either. If things get hectic just before opener, as usual, I'll just whip out my check-off list and be ready to go with all of my gear in no time. Naturally, I'll type the list on my computer, since I have always been known around these parts for at least one bad habit … my poor penmanship.

Plus, I'm heading to the deer shack early. I'll take care of those pesky chores so they won't cut into my hunting time like this year. I'll be ready and won't have to stay up half the night messing around to get the place in order.

That about sums it up! For next year's deer season I'll be well prepared. While the rest of the party is fumbling around and getting organized, I'll be in the woods hunting. And I'll be thinking about my next adventures and wondering where I put my fly rod. You see … I'm already looking forward to the fishing opener.